PREACHING THROUGH THE YEAR OF MATTHEW

SERMONS THAT WORK X

EDITORS

Roger Alling is president of the Episcopal Preaching Foundation, and director of the Foundation's widely acclaimed Preaching Excellence Program for students in Episcopal seminaries. He has edited each of the ten volumes in *Sermons that Work*, this anthology series committed to the celebration and nurture of preaching in the Episcopal tradition. He has been a parish priest and diocesan stewardship officer. Currently he serves as a priest associate in southwest Florida, and oversees the Foundation's new initiative of diocesan preaching conferences.

David J. Schlafer is a former philosophy professor and seminary subdean who has taught homiletics at four Episcopal seminaries and the College of Preachers. A faculty member of the D.Min. in Preaching Program at the Association of Chicago Theological Schools, he devotes primary energy to leading conferences on preaching across the United States, Canada, and England. He has written *Surviving the Sermon: A Guide to Preaching for Those Who Have to Listen*; *Your Way with God's Word: Discovering Your Distinctive Preaching Voice*; and *What Makes This Day Different: Preaching Grace on Special Occasions*.

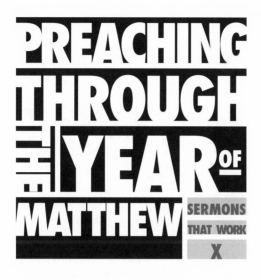

PREACHING THROUGH THE YEAR OF MATTHEW

SERMONS THAT WORK X

Edited by
Roger Alling and David J. Schlafer

MOREHOUSE PUBLISHING

© 2001 by Roger Alling and David J. Schlafer

Morehouse Publishing
P.O. Box 1321
Harrisburg, PA 17105

Morehouse Publishing is a division of The Morehouse Group.

Cover design by Trude Brummer

Library of Congress Cataloging-in-Publication Data
Preaching through the year of Matthew / edited by Roger Alling and David Schlafer
    p. cm. — (Sermons that work ; 10)
  Includes bibliographical references.
  ISBN 0-8192-1818-9 (alk. paper)
    1. Episcopal Church—Sermons. 2. Sermons, American. 3. Church year sermons. I. Alling, Roger, 1933–II. Schlafer, David J., 1944–III. Series.

BX5937 .A1 A4 2001
252'.0373—dc21   2001030673

Printed in the United States of America

01 02 03 04 05 9 8 7 6 5 4 3 2

Contents

3 Preaching Through the Season After Pentecost

4 Preparing to Preach—Homiletical Reflections

5 The Calling of the Preacher—Sermons in Celebration

Introduction

The Reign of God Is Like . . .

It is a warm spring day in early June. Warm, but not stuffy—the breeze is blowing. The lecture room is filled to capacity with folks who have come because they care about preaching: seminary students—participants in the annual Preaching Excellence Conference, conference staff, visitors who have gotten word that Barbara Brown Taylor has come to talk about "Preaching from/and to the Heart."

If you like, you can listen in, as well. She is already deeply into her presentation. The energy in the room is skipping and dancing:

> I have always thought that believers in the Word made flesh have an implicit duty to attend to physical details in the language they use. It is not enough to say what something means, without also disclosing how it looks, sounds, smells, tastes, and feels. If we can trust those details, then very often the meaning will take care of itself. One benefit of using such embodied language is that it wakes us up to the everyday parables going on all around us. Instead of tuning out so much of what goes on around us (because we have to get to work, have to return phone calls, have to get to the next appointment), we may tune into it instead. We may pay attention to all of the little dramas we generally walk right by: a mother with her sobbing child, a passionate argument going on in the car ahead of us in traffic, a highway median blooming with poppies and trash. We can stop, look, and listen, asking the same questions over and over again. What is going on here? What is this like? Where is God in this event?

Last year, my husband Ed decided that what we needed more than anything was a flock of guinea hens—those unreal-looking salt-and-pepper-colored birds with red wattles who make more racket than a pen full of beagles. His first batch of five lasted exactly one day after he let them loose in the yard. We figure that a weasel got them, since all three of the dogs swore that they were innocent. The second batch of five hens also lasted one day, so Ed built a big pen and kept the third batch in it for the better part of a year. The smell was—well, about what you would expect—but the hens survived.

Then a month ago, Ed let them out—and behold, they lived! They quickly took over the five acres around our house, flushing yellow moths from the long grass, and pecking at anything that moved. They also established a pecking order among themselves. Four of them got along fine, but they made life hell for the fifth. They chased her away from the cracked corn Ed pitched to them. They would not let her sit on the fence rail with them. Whatever was wrong with her was invisible to human eyes, but to guinea hen eyes, she was a real leper.

One evening I was down in the garden at dusk, which is when the guinea hens find a low branch to roost on for the night. They picked a young oak that night, right where the clover smell of the pasture meets the deep leaf smell of the woods. One by one, the first four guinea hens took off with a great beating of wings and huddled on the branch. As each one arrived, the others made room. Finally only the fifth one was left on the ground, but every time she rose to join them they beat her back, screaming at her as they rushed at her with their beaks. After six or seven tries she just stood in the wet grass below them and cried.

The next morning, four guinea hens strutted by my kitchen window. I looked everywhere for the fifth, but she was gone for good. I want to believe that she joined the flock down the road, but I don't think she could have made it that far all by herself. The woods around my house are full of predators—not only weasels but also coyotes and wild dogs. A guinea hen's protection is her flock, only her flock would not have her.

I am not sure how the parable ends, but there it is. I tried to tell it so that you could sense it, but I also tried not to process it too much for you. Instead of telling you how I felt, I tried to show you what made me feel how I felt. Then I left you alone to feel whatever you felt. If it worked, then you thought some things too—about human pecking orders, maybe, or about what happens when we refuse to roost with one another. I tried not to moralize. I just put the dots on the page and let you connect them, so that the conclusion was as much yours as mine.

I learned this straight from Jesus, who knew just when to end a story—often with a question—without wrapping it up too neatly. Did the elder brother ever accept his father's invitation to come to the party, or did he stand out in the yard hating his prodigal brother for the rest of his life? Why was the servant who buried his master's one talent punished for his prudence? Does God really prefer gamblers? What kind of boss pays those who come late to the vineyard the same as those who arrived at daybreak? If that is grace, then it is not fair.

Stories like these carry emotional punch as well as intellectual challenge, but Jesus seemed to know that they would work better if he let his listeners make their own discoveries. Not too long ago, someone came up to me after a sermon and said, "You sat down a little too soon for me." What he meant, I think, was that I did not bring the sermon to a satisfying conclusion for him, and while I have worried since then about letting him down, I try to remember that Jesus was always sitting down too soon for most people. People who asked him concrete questions got stories for answers. People who wanted him to settle things for them went away unsettled instead. Sometimes I wonder if he would have lasted as rector of a parish. Somehow I doubt it.

Meanwhile, I am not Jesus and neither are you. But we do want to follow him and we want to last. We also want to be heard, since we believe that it is not only we who speak, but God who speaks through us. Speaking to the heart is one way to go at it—speaking to the whole human being, by using embodied language that incarnates the gospel over and over again.

Barbara Taylor may not be *Jesus*. But perhaps she *is* a modern-day Matthew of sorts—wrestling, as all gospel bearers must, with what it means to find Spirit-freshness in words that are often disdained and discarded as flat and dead. Like Matthew, Barbara Taylor finds that ordinary words work just fine. They make good sense—good cognitive, good spiritual sense—so long as they are rubbed up against the real world they represent—then, set alongside one another in ways that spark, they send up flares that shed light on the heavens.

How does a preacher talk of heavenly things? "The kingdom of heaven is like . . ." says Matthew's Jesus—The Commonwealth of God is like—well—like *common things*. Things appreciated and held up, so folks can say: "Oh, goodness! Farmers, fishing nets, mustard seeds, wheat mixed up with weeds! Who could have imagined that God's reign would play like *that*? The Commonwealth of God, like a woman baking bread—imagine that! Imagine heaven as deeply buried treasure (rather dirty, when unearthed). Consider! The wealth of the kingdom as a pearl you must go bankrupt for!"

The Year of Matthew is an opportunity for preachers, like Barbara, Fred, Tashika, Chun Wei, Sally, and Ingrid, to savor afresh, and to share with others what they see, smell, and taste. Not just to "preach on Matthew's Gospel," but to share Matthew's penchant for sensing things live, and sharing them real. The Commonwealth of God may be *more* than a thousand common things. But it isn't one thing *less*.

As with previous volumes in this series, what is offered here is *not* the work of those who, by somebody's yardstick, measure up as towering preaching superstars—ones the rest of us can only *ooh* and *ah* up to. Here is daily bread, prayed for, kneaded, baked, and served. It is not intended to dazzle, but to nourish, and perhaps to delight as well. Welcome to the smorgasbord!

Some features from previous volumes in this series have been continued. In two cases (John's story about Jesus at the well with the woman of Samaria, and Matthew's Passion Gospel appointed for Palm Sunday), texts no less daunting to the preacher for being familiar, each receives two very different sermon treatments. Reading listeners are, again, offered the chance to overhear the Word of the Lord proclaimed in the worship rhythm of the Preaching Excellence Conference. The "pause for homiletical reflection" between sermons, for the Liturgical year, and sermons preached at the conference, has been continued as well. The distinguished contributors of these reflections are: Katharine Jefferts Schori, recently selected as chief pastor of the Episcopal Church in Nevada; and Eugene Lowry, preaching conference leader and Methodist professor of homiletics. In the final sermon of this volume, Barbara Brown Taylor returns, getting an opportunity to practice what she preaches.

The editors again thank Morehouse Publishing for their support of this venture.

SECOND SUNDAY OF ADVENT

Violence

Isaiah 11:1–10; Psalm 72; Romans 15:4–13; Matthew 3:1–12
Timothy E. Kimbrough

DO YOU remember the first violence done in the garden of Eden?

"Why start there?" you ask.

It is the place of our first being, the seat of innocence, an example of what was meant to be, and of what that became. To return to this story each Easter and Christmas, as we do in our Vigil readings, is to open the family album, looking for clues that might explain why we live as we do today, looking, as well, for a reason to hope.

So I ask again: Do you remember the first violence done in the garden of Eden? Cain killing his brother Abel? No. That happens a little later in Genesis.

The casting of Adam and Eve out of the garden, and the placing of sentries with flaming swords at the gates to prevent reentry? Well, that *is* a violence of sorts; but I'm not sure it's the *first* violence.

If you want to talk about the violence of lying and deception, then maybe you'd point to the exchange between Eve, the serpent, and Adam. But, I think, you run the risk of domesticating violence if you start there.

How about this: "And the LORD God made garments of skins for the man and for his wife, and clothed them." Initially Adam and Eve were naked without shame. But after eating the forbidden fruit, the urgency for clothing is apparent—first in a set of fig-leaf tights that Eve whips together, and then in animal skins that God provides for them before driving them out of the Garden. Vulnerability leads to shame, and shame to violence. An animal is killed to provide protection for Adam and Eve—protection from the elements, from the environment, and from one another. An animal is killed.

Tradition suggests that this animal was a lamb, thus drawing a straight line between the violence of Eden, the violence of Israel's cult of ritual sacrifice, and the violence of the cross of Christ, the Lamb of God who takes away the sin of the world.

Violence is present in the Garden of Eden after the Fall because it represents the way of the world. It represents how we are. It represents the manner in which a fallen world responds; how you respond when you are threatened, challenged, made vulnerable, and confronted by your own weaknesses. Nations go to war when sovereignty is threatened, or when additional land for protection is required. Terrorists engage in acts of random violence when they are cornered. Perpetrators of domestic violence, spousal abuse, and the beating of children often lash out against those around them because they themselves have been made vulnerable to such violence and abuse in their youth.

Society then engages security networks and the police, examples of socially sanctioned violence, to protect law-abiding citizens. And the state employs the death penalty as punishment and deterrent against the next capital crime.

If you can't see it in the world around you, Eden teaches you that violence is a way—the way—of life for us. From the food we eat, to the clothes we wear; from the wars we fight and fund, to the law enforcement officers we invite into our homes and communities; from the land we presume to own, wrested from those who went before us, to the neighborhoods we designate as safe and unsafe—violence is the way of life for us, and a primary marker of sin.

Yet all the preparing, and watching, and waiting we are asked to do during this season of Advent is informed by the prophets' shout: The Reign of God, when it comes, will be characterized by the absence of violence.

Isaiah writes: "The wolf shall dwell with the lamb, and the leopard shall lie down with the kid, and the calf and the lion and the fatling together, and a little child shall lead them. The cow and the bear shall feed; their young shall lie down together; and the lion shall eat straw like the ox. The sucking child shall play over the hole of the asp, and the weaned child shall put his hand on the adder's den. They shall not hurt or destroy in all my holy mountain." Paul exhorts the Christians in Rome to live in harmony with one another and prays that "the God of hope fill you with all joy and peace." And the Psalmist sings that "in his days may righteousness flourish and peace abound, until the moon is no more." Such images are as unthinkable as the beating of swords into plowshares. They are beyond what we can imagine. In fact, they are beyond the desire of our hearts, so ingrained is this way of violence.

Do you have trouble considering what the church means when it speaks of Original Sin? Think of it in terms of violence, and perhaps you will recognize a marker of humanity's flawed nature. Some will turn their heads indignantly and suggest they eschew violence of all kinds. And yet, no matter whether you are a vegetarian or a member of People for the Ethical Treatment of Animals (PETA), the Episcopal Peace Fellowship, or the Sierra Club, you cannot divorce yourself from a society that hallows the electric chair, firing squads, and hypodermic needles.

John the Baptist points his finger at the Pharisees and Sadducees who have come to him for baptism without having repented of their sin. He despairs. They have refused to renounce a system of worship that does not seek the reform of heart and the reform of society. "You brood of vipers!" he shouts, ". . . [b]ear fruit that befits repentance, and do not presume to say to yourselves, 'We have Abraham as our father.'" When he prophesies against them, he is shouting at a world that has refused to embrace the hope of the prophets, refused to see sin in their violence, and refused to kneel before the mountain of the Lord.

The Kingdom of God will be like this: not as you expected. Neither the violent, nor the powerful, nor the politically astute will hold sway in the Kingdom of God. No. The first will be last and the last first. And who are our last? The poor, the imprisoned, the victims of their crimes, the dead by capital punishment, the sick, the lonely, the disenfranchised, the victims of racism and social prejudice of every kind. The first will be last and the last first. The wolf and lamb will lie down together. Swords will be beat into plowshares, and pedigree will count for nothing.

This is the gospel of the prophets, the gospel of John the Baptist, and the gospel of Jesus Christ. Turn and repent from every way that sustains the first, the elite. Stand with the last. Love the last, the least, the lost, and the forgotten, and so anticipate the Reign of God.

Now, I realize, it is hard to preach this gospel with Bing Crosby (as much as I love him) singing, "It's beginning to look a lot like Christmas, everywhere I go." Why? Because if the coming of the Prince of Peace looked like the prophets describe it, then it would mean the end of the world as I know it. And that is simply more than I can take. I love life like it is too much.

So does the world. Every time someone comes preaching this gospel we kill him. We isolated the great prophets of the Old Testament. John the Baptist was beheaded. Jesus, crucified. Stephen, the Deacon, stoned to death.

And we still kill them. Take someone like Martin Luther King, Jr., assassinated for his vision and proclamation of the Kingdom of God. Take someone like Oscar Romero, archbishop of El Salvador in the 1970s, assassinated by government troops during mass one day for his work as a fearless defender of the poor, the suffering, and the tortured in his society. He preached the gospel of Jesus Christ and gave his life for it.

When you look around you see the church in conflict with itself and with the world around it. Do not despair. Better, *conflict* with the forces of this world and of evil than *complicity* with them.

Over twenty years ago Archbishop Romero, speaking to the role of the church in society, included the following words in an Advent homily to his flock: "This is why the church has great conflicts: It accuses of sin. It says to the rich: 'Do not sin by misusing your money.' It says to the powerful: 'Do not misuse your political influence. Do not misuse your weaponry. Do not misuse your power. Don't you see that is a sin?' It says to sinful torturers: 'Do not torture. You are sinning. You are doing wrong. You are establishing the reign of hell on earth.'"[1]

As newspapers, radio programs, and the evening news bring us the promise of economic bonanza for merchants, and as they continue to chart the remaining shopping days until Christmas, do not forget to give this gospel equal time. John the Baptist's call to repentance is a call to acknowledge the violence of sin in our lives, and a call to turn from that.

The coming of the Prince of Peace and the vision of Isaiah's holy mountain are going to turn your world upside down. You can either ignore the prophecy and deny its truth, or embrace it and continue your pilgrimage of repentance, ascending the holy mountain of God.

Lamb of God, you take away the sin of the world: have mercy on us.
Lamb of God, you take away the sin of the world: have mercy on us.
Lamb of God, you take away the sin of the world: grant us peace.

Timothy E. Kimbrough is rector of the Church of the Holy Family, Chapel Hill, North Carolina.

---

1. James R. Brockman, *The Violence of Love: the Pastoral Wisdom of Archbishop Oscar Romero* (San Francisco: Harper & Row, 1988), p. 19.

FOURTH SUNDAY OF ADVENT

Joseph's Cross

Matthew 1:18–25
Catherine Woods Richardson

IMAGINE HOW you'd feel.

Your fiancée tells you she's pregnant, and you know you had nothing to do with it. She's got some cockamamie explanation that really doesn't make sense; and even in the face of certain disgrace, she doesn't seem ashamed. Instead, she looks more radiant than you've ever seen her. It feels like a kick in the gut.

You're confused and hurt, and you don't know what to do. No matter what the truth is, people will blame you. They'll whisper and avoid you on the street, take their business somewhere else. You're a good man; you've tried hard to do what's right by your family and fiancée, and now this. Betrayal. You'll never live this down, and you didn't even do anything wrong.

Human life is messy. And I think one of the truths of this Advent and Christmas season, once we get past all the hype and sentiment of commerce, is that sometimes God comes along in our messy human lives and makes them a whole lot messier. Gee, thanks, God.

Jesus' conception completely overturns Mary and Joseph's lives. Jesus was born in a time when, at best, unmarried parents faced certain social disgrace. At worst, unfaithful women could be stoned to death for adultery. This new babe growing in Mary's womb is a burden indeed. No one has asked for this to happen, least of all Joseph. Joseph is stuck between a rock and a hard place. There is no good decision for him to make when he learns of Mary's pregnancy.

I think many of us find ourselves in Joseph's shoes, one time or another. I don't mean in dealing with another's mysterious pregnancy, at least in a literal sense, but in finding the spark of God growing in someone to whom we're promised, changing him in ways we'd never planned or imagined. Upsetting our own lives. It can be disorienting and deeply painful. It can feel like betrayal—the spouse who wants to change careers, once we've finally got things in order; the child who leaves the church, or drops out of college; the friends or siblings we feel so distant from, now that our lives have taken different paths. When people we love change in unexpected ways, it can be very hard—even harder than when we ourselves change.

When *we're* growing in God, we may at least know a bit of what is going on. But family and friends often know much less; and they can feel cast off and abandoned, as we enter into the mystery of God's workings. God doesn't promise that our lives will be neat and tidy, that they will be free of conflict or tension or uncertainty.

Joseph never would have said that God plays fair. After all, he was a righteous man, not looking for any trouble—and look what he gets! Before he has fully decided what to do about Mary's news, he sleeps on it. An angel of the Lord appears to him, saying, "Joseph, son of David, do not be afraid to take Mary as your wife, for the child conceived in her is from the Holy Spirit." These do not sound like reassuring words. An illegitimate child of uncertain parentage is bad enough, but now the angel says it's not even an ordinarily conceived human child, but something conceived from the Holy Spirit. *What* on earth will *that* turn out to be?

The angel says, "Don't be afraid"? Yeah, right. Try "terrified" instead. Things were bad enough before this news. Whatever happened to a nice, quiet life in Nazareth?

God didn't give Jesus a nice, quiet life in Nazareth, and he didn't give it to Mary and Joseph either. All three of them bore their crosses—Jesus' was of wood, but Mary and Joseph's cross was Jesus himself. It is no small task to be a human father to God incarnate.

It is no small task, but it is an awesome and wondrous one, and surely Joseph knew it. Joseph was a righteous man, a faithful Jew. Could anyone less be blessed and burdened with such amazing news as Mary had to share? Could anyone less have borne the consequences?

In the collect for this last Sunday of Advent, we pray: "Purify our conscience, Almighty God, by your daily visitation, that your Son Jesus Christ, at his coming, may find in us a mansion prepared for himself." This collect, and the example of Mary, the Mother of God, reminds us of our call to be Godbearers, to carry and bring to life the spark of God in a suffering world.

But this Sunday, too, as we hear Joseph's story, we are reminded that we are also called to be companions to the ones in whom the spark of God is growing. This may be a harder task yet, to welcome God's transforming work in the lives of those closest to us, as they change and grow into new and different people before our very eyes.

But there are rewards. When we join Joseph in accompanying another who carries Christ within, we can find ourselves, some cold, dark night, as midwives to the greatest power of this world. We can be struck to awe-filled silence by the wonder of God's love embodied in this person we thought we knew so well. We can hold the Christ child in our arms.

Will this be messy? Sure. Will it hurt? It will likely break our hearts and souls wide open. Will it be the most amazing, awesome, and wonderful thing we could ever do? Yes, that too. In these last days of Advent, let us join Joseph and go look for Mary. And when we've found her, and told her we're still here, let us set out together on the road to Bethlehem. Let us walk these dwindling days to the place where God is born.

Catherine Woods Richardson is interim pastor of
St. Paul's Church, Elk City, Michigan.

CHRISTMAS EVE

The Most Special Effect of All

Luke 2:1–20
Matthew R. Lincoln

WHEN YOU see a blockbuster movie these days, some of the key ingredients are sure to be the special effects. The effects sometimes do more to attract an audience than the starring actors. When I was a kid, watching special effects was often amusing, rather than scary. It was easy to tell that the ship being blown up was just a boat in a bathtub.

It is still fun, but detecting the special effects is now more of a challenge, a kind of game. You want the effects to be believable; but you know they can't be what they appear to be, and because of that knowledge, you can gauge how convincing the special effects are. A really satisfying effect is one that you can say was convincing. The irony is, however, if it had *really* been convincing, you wouldn't have recognized that it was only an effect. You wouldn't be sitting back and *deciding* whether or not it was convincing; you would simply be *convinced*.

We like our special effects to be big and bold, but somehow, visibly unreal. They are safer that way. Being terrified by them is only an amusement.

Is that how you would like God to be? Would you like God only to *look* almighty—that is, to look spectacular while, in fact, being *safely unreal*? That would have advantages. The spectacle would give us something to get excited about; but we would be left to ourselves to decide what we care about, and how we want to spend our lives.

7

Have you ever wanted God to make a real difference in your life, such as when you or someone you love was gravely ill? You pray for a miracle cure, or a rescue from trouble—a zap from a distant, impersonal God that will put things back the way they were. Such a dramatic act by an impersonal God would seem to be powerful, like a special effect. But such an act would not really change anything.

On a movie screen, a great huge ship can hit an iceberg and sink at 1, 3, 5, 7 and 9 P.M. (with senior citizen discounts at the early shows); then do it again five times on the following day. You feel scared while you watch, but nothing changes. An impersonal God might be talked into doing something for you, like a cure. But that cure would do nothing except return things to normal. If your life is in chaos because of an illness, "normal" sounds pretty good. But think about it. Would you really like things to go right back to where they were, with you about to get sick all over again?

"Then an angel of the Lord stood before them, and the glory of the Lord shone around them." Quite a special effect, wouldn't you say? ". . . [A]nd they were terrified. But the angel said, to them, 'Do not be afraid; for see—I am bringing you good news of great joy for all the people.'"

And what was the good news? That God is *not* like an angel. That God has come, not as a spirit, not a special effect—unreal and impersonal.

God is very personal. So personal that he came with a person's name. In the Greek that was spoken in his day and in his country, his name was Jesus. In the original language of his people, Hebrew, it was simply Joshua, a meaningful name, but not uncommon. Except for the angels, he came with no special effects. No one would have discovered him, even by accident, if the angelic host had not burst upon the shepherds in their field and sent them to Bethlehem.

The way God comes to us is easy to miss, but very personal—the opposite of a special effect. Unlike a special effect that appears to be dramatic and powerful but changes nothing, God slips into our lives in a small, seemingly insignificant way—a newborn baby—and changes everything.

Ask any parents about the arrival of a newborn. Now, chances are, they'll tell you their baby came with all kinds of special effects, but I can tell you their neighbors may not even know there is a new baby next door. No, the stories new parents want to tell about the baby's birth really just say that now, everything is different. The presence of the new baby changes everything. That is what they are trying to say.

It is no accident or happpenstance that God came into the world as a baby. He had come in other ways before: the three angels who appeared to Abraham, the pillar of cloud by day and fire by night that led the Israelites in the wilderness, a still, small voice heard by Elijah, an ineffable presence in the inner sanctuary, the Holy of Holies of the Temple in Jerusalem.

But God chose to come into the world to reveal himself fully and completely as a person, one who started out life in the same way every other real person ever has or ever will. We often think of the adult Jesus as a prophet, teacher, or role model. He was all of those and more. We often think of that adult Jesus as the "real" Jesus, the important Jesus. But the two most important things he ever did were to be born, and to die. His birth and his death mean at least this: God lived your life. His death means more than that, as well, but tonight, on Christmas Eve, his death is taken together with his birth.

God lived a mortal life like yours. And he did it that way because he wanted to be part of your life. He did it that way so that you won't go away from an encounter with him the way you might leave a block-buster movie, shaking your head in wonder at the special effects, but otherwise unchanged. He did it that way so that when you do go away from an encounter with him, you know that God has been with you, really, personally, and that you have been changed.

If you have some illness that needs to be healed, some situation in which all your options have become dead ends, pray for God to help you. But do so knowing that God will not be satisfied by simply returning things to the way they were. He will take you through to a new way of being. For God was born into our life so that we might grow into the people he made us to be. He made us in his image, to grow into his likeness. We begin that growth the moment we're born, and never cease to grow towards him. He came to us, so that we might grow towards him.

Do not be afraid. The Good News is that God is not an impersonal angel, but became a very real person, born to live your life, and to change it forever.

Matthew R. Lincoln is rector of St. John's Church,
North Haven, Connecticut.

Family Identity

Matthew 3:13–17
Cecilia Bliley Duke

BEFORE ENTERING seminary, I was an elementary school counselor. From time to time, I was required to take courses in order to renew my certification. One year I took a class that addressed the problems of child abuse and neglect. To my surprise, there was another counselor in the class named Cecilia. Not long after the class began, Cecilia confided in me that she was worried about the teenage girl who was baby-sitting her children. The baby sitter always seemed anxious and agitated. She was withdrawn and nervous. She could barely hold her head up to look at Cecilia in conversation.

Cecilia noticed the baby sitter was always eager to come to her house. She never spoke of her own family. She was a good student and loved to run track, but she didn't seem to have the normal life of a teenager: no friends, no phone calls, no interest in clothes, no trips to the mall. Though she was shy and withdrawn, she enjoyed playing with Cecilia's children.

One day, as Cecilia rushed out the door to class, she inadvertently left one of her books on the counter in the kitchen. It was a book about child abuse. When she came home that night, the baby sitter met her at the door. Looking troubled and shaken, she asked Cecilia if they could talk for a few minutes.

Into the late hours of the night, this girl poured out her heart. When she was only two, her parents had divorced. She and her three brothers continued to live with their mother, and the father moved away. When she was nine, her mother died suddenly, and the children went to live with their father and his new wife.

Life with her stepmother was horrible, she said. Coldness and conflict were the rule of life in her home. Her father retreated from it all by working from early dawn until late at night. While he was gone, her stepmother would actually lock herself in her room to be away from the children. The girl's life crumbled into chaos. One of her older brothers began to abuse her sexually. She was filled with shame and fear. She felt different from other kids. She had no one to talk to.

All this she emptied out to Cecilia that night. As a professional counselor, Cecilia knew she would have to report the story to the Department of Family and Children's Services, as mandated by state law. But how would her baby sitter feel about this disclosure? Would she feel betrayed?

To Cecilia's surprise, her young friend was actually relieved. Things had gotten so bad for her that any change would be an improvement. The baby sitter was only one month from her eighteenth birthday, so the Department opted to let her stay in her home until she could legally leave on her own. But where could she go? She had four months of high school left. If she left her father and stepmother, she would forfeit all of her financial support.

At this turning point, Cecilia and her husband and children performed an act of love and faith. They became their baby sitter's legal guardians. They assumed responsibility for her education, her health insurance, and her emotional and physical well-being.

Cecilia would tell you that including this young person in the circle of her family was not easy. She brought with her many challenging and complex problems. But little by little, she was able to refashion a life for herself. With a few false starts, and many bumps and scrapes, she found a sense of identity, self-esteem, and freedom.

Now she is a young adult. She has graduated from college and become a teacher of children with special emotional needs. Though she keeps in close touch with her adopted family, she lives independently, and is making friends.

What was it that made the difference for her? Finding a family—a place to belong.

Today's story in Matthew's Gospel tells of Jesus' baptism. There, standing along the banks of the Jordan, a group of bystanders, people like you and me, people like Cecilia and her baby sitter, witness the remarkable revelation of Jesus' identity as the Son of God. Why is this event important to them? Why is it important to the community wherein Matthew is writing? What difference does it make to us?

Jesus' baptism marks his true identity, his kinship with God—a kinship that propels Jesus to obey the call to love. This call takes him along the dusty road of Palestine, touching and healing the bruised and the weak. It takes him into the political arena, where he will know the public shame and the physical agony of being stripped and crucified. It takes him to the grave, wherein he conquers death, and rises into communion with God.

In answering this call, Jesus opens up the way for us. He extends the boundaries of God to include us as a family—a kinship that saves us and gives us our true identity. Christ's obedience to the call of love means that we no longer have to live in isolation, fear, and loneliness. We have a place. We belong. Through Christ and through our own baptism, we now live in a family, the family of God. And if we are family, that means we are siblings of Christ and siblings of each other. In some ways, this is good news, but in another way, it is troubling news.

If we're siblings, that means we have to look out for each other. We can't just run off to our private rooms, like the stepmother did. If we are truly family, we gather together in the *living* room. It's in the living room—our shared community—that we work out our squabbles and rivalries. We comfort the one who loses a friend. We nurse the one who is too sick to work. We share with the one who is too poor to feed herself. We protect the young ones who are defenseless. We guard the one who is subject to hurt. And we celebrate with the one who achieves the goal or earns the prize.

The boundaries of God's family don't stop here in this small community— or even in the larger church. The boundaries encompass all—the starving child in Sudan, the vicious military dictator, the victims of hurricanes, human injustice, and violence. If we are all related, then what we do affects everyone else in the family. And if we obey the call to love, which our baptism requires, then we cannot ignore the trouble in our family.

As complicated as our family seems, it is hard to know where to start. It's hard to know how to care without getting swallowed up and overwhelmed. Yet, I think that God unfolds the way for us, if we remain open. The specific focus of our call to love at any given moment eventually emerges as we pray. This openness to our source affirms our identity, our belonging, our sense of being loved. Out of that identity, we can love in just the places where we are needed. We can live mindful of the deprivation that others feel when we take too much. We can listen to our enemies and create new ways to live cooperatively. But only in our *kinship with God* can we hope to do this.

A few weeks ago, I had lunch with Cecilia's baby sitter. Toward the end of the meal, she took from her pocket a picture of herself as a young child, sitting on her mother's lap. One of her aunts had saved it for her. She looked admiringly at the picture. She told me that she wants to get to know her mother. She is going to visit extended family to learn as much about her as she can. She wants to explore her memories.

Perhaps that is what our prayer is: getting to know ourselves in God, sharing our extended family, until we reach the source that sustains us and empowers us to obey the call to love in our family of God.

Cecilia Bliley Duke is associate rector of St. Patrick's Church, Atlanta, Georgia.

If That's Not God

Isaiah 49:1–7
Richard J. Jones

WE HAVE come to worship God at the start of the semester. Even on this first day of classes, though some white squares still remain on our personal calendars like precious patches of unblemished snow, you and I know that there is more work coming up than there will be time and energy to do. One leafing through the ethics syllabus, one stroll past the reserve shelves and the current periodicals is enough to convince me that information overload is already upon us.

Overload is not just a feature of the educational enterprise, of course. *Life* overloads. There are more wars going on than the secretary general of the United Nations can monitor. There are more cases pending than the Alexandria Circuit Court can adjudicate. There are definitely more household chores outstanding than I can get done.

Conventional wisdom says: *Select!* You can't do it all, so choose some part. Prioritize. Specialize. It's better to do one thing well than ten poorly.

And this conventional wisdom produces results. The Industrial Revolution made a virtue of specialization. Specialization has made us collectively rich in goods, services, and information. Likewise in academia: scholars can go deeper because they do not try to cover all subjects. So in the parish: leaders accomplish more when they confine their efforts to stated areas. Specialization gives. But specialization also takes away.

Narrowing our focus liberates, but narrowing our focus also robs us. Production line workers get bored and careless. Bureaucrats become insulated inside their own expertise. The sealed community that shuts out the unmanageable begins to find itself breathing stale air. We must specialize to survive. But, by specializing, we lose touch.

Second Isaiah, the Prophet of the Exile, speaks for God to a community that knew it was coping with overload. Israel's world of meaning had been shattered at the destruction of the Temple, the fall of the House of David, and the deporting of priests and leaders to Babylon. How to cope, in a place where foreign languages seemed to be the ladder to success? Where Bel, Nebo, and other rivals of the God of Israel seemed to deliver protection?

The core of the exile community responded by narrowing its focus. The community resisted being dissipated or assimilated. And so this faithful, focused, inner-directed community of Jews in Babylon would have been ready to hear the word: that God, in mercy, was now going to restore the structures that would keep the foreign floods from overwhelming them. The Prophet of the Exile was perhaps prepared to focus on the restoring of something ancestral and familiar: the old tribal structure of Israel.

So I imagine the word of the Lord coming to Second Isaiah as something of a surprise: "It is too light a thing that you should be my servant to raise up the tribes of Jacob and to restore the preserved of Israel. *I will give you as a light to the nations, that my salvation may reach to the end of the earth.*"

To the nations? What about our own fragmented nation? To the end of the earth? What about focus?

The Word, however, is insistent. "It is too light a thing that you should be my servant only to restore Israel—chosen, loved, and holy though Israel may be. The wisdom of common experience may have convinced you that sanity and survival require you to specialize. You are, indeed, to be commended for surviving this far—for having focused enough to ward off the unmanageable. But now I am telling you something new. My salvation involves something wider than your survival. I am the Creator of all, the God of all nations. My salvation is to reach to the end of the world. And you, my focused servant, are now to begin to shine your light outward."

If you see where I am heading, you may well be starting to get up your resistance at this point. Israel certainly resisted. What kind of Prophet of Consolation is he who tells exiled people to give up the inward focus that is the very thing that has saved them from alien overload? Why is it too light a thing to be a disciplined student, cultivating one's recognized gifts? What is too light about becoming a faithful pastor and seeking to build up or restore one congregation? What kind of heavy God would expect us to take on the ancient feuds of the Serbs and the Croats? What kind of heavy God would assign us a role in the survival of the church in Sudan, now suffering in the third decade of an ethnic and religious civil war? What will happen to us if we say Yes! to this word that says God's saving activity extends to the end of the earth? What will happen if our focus is so unbearably broadened? Who are we to be burdened with this light to the nations?

We may become *bearers* of the light, but we are *not* the light. That is the Good News. In Jesus Christ, God's light has beamed, once and for all, unmistakably and inextinguishably, through the world's darkness. The obedience that even the chosen people could not render, even prodded by the prophets—this obedience Jesus Christ *did* render. And the powers of darkness that appear to control the world were seen by the light of Easter

Day to be defeated. So the light is now shining. Around the world, more than two billion living persons have seen the light of Christ, and are now bearing that light. If we become bearers, we do not bear the light alone.

Moreover, fellow human bearers of the light of Christ are not our only companions. God, by the ongoing, unceasing work of the Spirit, is at work making himself known. I offer two examples of God currently at work among the nations.

Brazil is a country of great wealth, unevenly distributed. Its large cities of Rio de Janeiro, São Paulo, and Recife have become so swollen with poor people that some observers predict they will soon be sending waves of emigrants to the United States. Many despair.

Kosuke Koyama, professor of mission at Union Theological Seminary, New York, reports that "in a Recife slum, a woman said to a nun: 'Sister, today God has been to my house!' The nun asked how this was. She was told: 'I had no money to buy medicine for my little boy who is ill. Then my neighbor was paid for a whole week's washing—one hundred cruzeiros. She gave it all to me so that I could buy the medicine. If that's not God, what is?"[1] The God of mercy is making himself known daily, in Recife. It helps when there is a witness on the scene who can say, "Yes, that was the mercy of God. I, too, recognize that mercy in this event."

My second example of God manifesting himself in the world is from Africa. Three decades of war, pitting Nilotic southern Sudanese against an Islamic and Arab-dominated central government, have threatened cattle-herding groups like the Dinka with extinction. For generations the Dinka looked down on more urbanized and Christianized groups, until the present war deprived them of pastureland, livestock, and men. In the last few years, many Dinka have lost faith in the traditional gods whom they once thought protected them. According to the late Marc Nikkel, a missionary teacher in the southern Sudan war zone, in the past three years tens of thousands of Dinka women and men have burned their traditional shrines and erected crosses in their place. These Dinka are not seeking schooling or food or social prestige; they are simply seeking to survive. In a homestead of the nomadic Dinka, the center post of the thatched cattle shed is the most permanent structure. Nikkel reported the words of a song the Dinka are singing at the present time: "The cross on which Christ was nailed; it is the center post of the cattle shed. This cross now stands between the believer and the gods who formerly deceived us."[2]

The Spirit of God is at work in what might be called a people movement, or a group conversion process, going on in southern Sudan. It helps that teachers are present among the newly baptized Dinka who can offer to tell more of the story behind the cross that the Dinka have proudly erected.

To acknowledge that God's salvation reaches to the end of the earth may or may not involve my personally being called by God to work outside my focal area, outside my home culture. God may call us to raise up our own tribe. God may send us to another tribe. That is a matter for discernment, listening to the need of the church and the needs of the world.

But to know that God's salvation reaches to the end of the earth means at least this: I can never rest with the notion that God is interested only in us and ours. Of course God has known me from my mother's womb. God has had a hand on the servant at every step. But God does not limit himself to us. God does not have to screen out the alien, as we, coping with overload, are inclined to do. No nation is foreign to God. God meshes the curriculum into our vita, meshes our life into the life of others near and far.

To be a light to the nations could mean something so simple as this: to take note of the Spirit of God working in the lives of other people, and say: "If that's not God, what is?"

Richard J. Jones is professor of mission and world religions at Virginia Theological Seminary, Alexandria, Virginia.

1. Werner Ustorf in Frances Young, *Dare We Speak of God in Public?* (Mowbray, 1995,) p. 109.

2. Marc R. Nikkel, "The Cross of Bor Dinka Christians: a Working Christology in the Face of Displacement and Death," *Studies in World Christianity*, I (1995) (altered).

FOURTH SUNDAY AFTER THE EPIPHANY

The Beatitudes: *Is* or *Ought*?

Matthew 5:1–12
Malcolm Young

RUNNING ALONG the beach at night in Santa Monica, California, I was young and strong, feeling perfect exhilaration. Everything looked indistinct, without color, in the gray light under the blue-black sky. All I could hear was the sound of many waters rushing over the sand. Up ahead I saw a large log, rolling up and down the beach on its way to being swept out to sea.

As I ran closer, the edges of the log began to look more ragged, until I realized that it was a person caught in the undertow. Rushing out into the water, I somehow managed to bring the coughing, choking man to shore. He was wearing four different layers of torn, dirty clothing, and he smelled like bitter old wine.

Although later I looked around the boardwalk for a man wearing the old sweatshirt that I had given him, I never saw him again. I don't know whether his being in the water was the result of a deliberate effort to commit suicide, or an accident attributable to drunken stupor. I don't know his name or his story, his past or his future. I *do* know that life seemed to have damaged his soul. He seemed poor in spirit. It looked as though he mourned. Was this homeless man *blessed*?

Blessed are the poor in spirit. Blessed are those who mourn. Blessed are the meek, the merciful, those who hunger for righteousness and peace. Blessed are the persecuted. Are these memorable phrases true, or is Jesus merely making a virtue out of the bitter necessity of human suffering? The Good News in this Gospel is not obvious. Some of us have already concluded that meek guys finish last.

The Beatitudes are among the most famous words that Christ spoke, and the most difficult. They lie close to the heart of the Christian message. But what do they mean? What are their consequences for us? Should we strive to be mournful or poor in spirit in the same sort of way that we try to be merciful peacemakers? I am going to suggest three ways of approaching these questions. I will speak about the nature of dissatisfaction, about the nature of the statements themselves, and about the prospect of our being transformed by the Beatitudes.

The word *beatitude* comes from a Latin word "beatus." In the Bible the Greek word means literally "blessed" or "happy." Happy are the poor in spirit, the meek, the pure in heart. In ordinary life we act on the expectation that the rich, the powerful, the popular, and the beautiful are happy. Usually when we are trying to be happy we are attempting in some way to become one of these. Perhaps this is why "Blessed are those who mourn" can sound so jarring. Perhaps this is why we do not go around telling the poor and homeless that "theirs is the kingdom of heaven."

The truly shocking thing is this, however: The kind of happiness to which we devote most of our energies and our hopes may have nothing to do with God's blessing. This may be disturbing, but it should not be entirely unfamiliar. If you have been human for very long, you have already begun to discover this simple but not obvious fact: "Having it all" is *not* having it *all*. Some of you know this from personal experience. It is part of why you may be here today.

Four years ago I was doing premarital counseling with a young couple who had met and fallen in love at the bank where they worked together. They were self-confident, good-looking, educated, and successful. Our meetings were going great until about two months before the wedding, when the groom's parents gave them a gift—half a million dollars to buy a house next door to local superstar athletes in the city's most glamorous suburb. But as a condition of the gift, the groom's parents insisted on a prenuptial agreement ensuring that their future daughter-in-law could never have a claim on the property.

The once harmonious counseling sessions suddenly became a battleground of deadly acrimony and debilitating insecurity. The groom's sensitivity and the bride's self-confidence completely dissolved. Despite all their suffering, the couple did not understand how a naïve priest like me could even suggest that the gift might not be worth it. I understand a little better today why Jesus says, "Blessed are the meek."

Not only do we want what God may not want for us; what we want may not even make us happy. Our desires to assert ourselves can cause misery to the very people we love the most. But this conclusion does not solve our problem. While the things we strive for may not bring us God's blessings, this does not prove that poverty of spirit *will*. Indeed the claim Jesus makes is stronger than this. What could it mean that those who mourn and are poor in spirit are blessed?

To explore this question I did some research in theology libraries. I read other sermons that had been preached on this question. A number of these sermons tried to explain away my discomfort by drawing the distinction between *is* and *ought*. They strongly asserted that Jesus is not asking his disciples to strive for poverty of spirit, or to mourn, as if these were moral goals. Instead, they claimed, Jesus is stating a fact about God's nature. We worship a God who loves and cares for the suffering, the persecuted, and the just. According to them, the Beatitudes are not moral exhortations, wise advice, or a reminder of our shortcomings, but rather the description of a God who is passionately concerned for the weak and suffering.

At first I found this conclusion satisfying. God cares. The bar of required moral effort is *not* impossibly high, after all, I thought. There is hope—even for me. I felt satisfied and comfortable instead of challenged. The feeling did not last. I went back to the Bible, to the Sermon on the Mount, and looked at all that follows the Beatitudes. The rest of Jesus' sermon has so many oughts in it, I soon realized that these other preachers had made a hard teaching too easy.

After the Beatitudes, Jesus speaks about our becoming the salt of the earth, the light of the world, a people in whom God's glory shines. What follows are moral proscriptions about every aspect of how we live, filled with commandments about loving enemies, cutting off sinful eyes and hands. These finally conclude with Jesus saying we are to, "[b]e perfect, therefore, [even] as [our] heavenly Father is perfect"(Matt. 5:48). Jesus has higher standards and greater plans for us than to merely reassure us about God's love. Any easy distinction allowing us to take comfort in facts without considering how we ought to live in light of those facts has no place in God's Kingdom.

If that is so, what prospects for transformation do we have? During World War II, C. S. Lewis gave a radio talk about whether Christianity is hard or easy.[1] Ultimately he concluded that it is both. Jesus says: "Take up [your] cross" (which is equivalent to being tortured to death, Matt. 16:24). But he also says: "My yoke is easy and my burden is light" (Matt. 11:30).

Being a Christian is tremendously *difficult* if you believe that you can be a Christian and remain who you are with your identity intact. Being a Christian is impossibly hard if we try to have something left over for ourselves after giving something to God. God is not asking for our time, our money, our labor, but for *us*. As long as we look at what God requires as something we do, instead of someone we are called to be, Christianity will seem to be impossible. God is radical enough to ask for everything.

Christianity is *easy*, though, because we were created for just this sort of transformation. We were made to become like Christ. We will never be happy with half-million-dollar homes, popularity, or extraordinary health and beauty because, quite simply, we were not created to be satisfied by these things. The vast desires we feel in our hearts can only find contentment in the depths of God. The Bible says that all things will be gathered together in Christ. Becoming anything else only isolates us from the source of all love.

The Beatitudes are both an impossible standard and a comforting word. When Jesus says blessed are the meek, the poor in spirit, those who mourn, and those who hunger for justice, *he* was all of these things. And *we* are to be like him. Jesus was vulnerable. He was willing to be part of this risky life. He was wounded by the likes of you and me. He was killed by a callous human culture, and was raised so that we could share that resurrected life.

Malcolm Young is assisting priest at St. Anne's Church,
Lincoln, Massachusetts.

---

1. C.S. Lewis, *Mere Christianity* (New York: Macmillan & Co., 1943), p. 166.

Righteous Cooking

1 Corinthians 2:1–11; Matthew 5:13–20
R. Bruce Birdsey

MY WIFE Brenda was out of town several days this past week. One day while she was gone, I got in the mood for beef stew, and decided, "I'll make it." Now, I am not a cook. I am a recipe follower. I looked up a recipe, bought the right ingredients, followed the directions, measured carefully. I did what the book said. And the result was—well, the result wasn't all that great, because I'm just not a cook. I don't have the instincts, the flair, the *je ne sais quoi* to be, in the kitchen, anything more than a recipe follower.

My wife is a cook. When she makes a dish, she may or may not refer to a recipe. The cookbook is a ready reference, in case the dish is one she's never made before. But it's only that, a reference, a loose structure. It's a ballpark in which she freely plays. She may add things the recipe doesn't call for. She may leave out things the recipe does call for. She uses the basic rules of cookery that she has become familiar with through long experience. But she interprets and improvises, using her good sense, her creative intuition, her taste buds, and her native appreciation of food. She doesn't violate the basic rules of cookery. She just works freely and easily within them, like an artist, and produces a very delicious result.

I could say to her, "Look, my beef stew is textbook. It has exactly the right amount of exactly every ingredient put together in exactly the right way." And then she could say to me, "Yeah, but mine tastes better."

The Pharisees, who get such bad press in the New Testament, weren't bad people. At their best, they were good people. But at times they could be rigorous recipe followers, doing things according to the book—even if the book seemed at odds with the realities of a human situation. As the Gospel writers often present them, the Pharisees tended to follow directions to the letter. They used the called-for ingredients. They measured carefully. But the result, while textbook, was sometimes not a tasty dish. Their piety, like my cooking, was sort of—forgettable.

Jesus was a cook. One Sabbath he was in the synagogue, and there was a man there with a crippled leg. He said to Jesus, "Please—heal me." And Jesus did. The Pharisees said, "Hey, you broke a rule. You ignored directions. The Law of Moses, our ultimate cookbook, says you can't do that on the Sabbath." They were recipe followers. Jesus said, "Look at the result. This man who's been crippled for years just now threw away his crutches, and walked out of here without a limp. Is that not a delicious dish, fit for the Sabbath? *Especially* for the Sabbath?"

As followers of Jesus our calling, our vocation, is to offer good nourishment to those around us, both near and far. "You are the salt of the earth," Jesus says. "You are the light of the world. Let your light shine." He would have us awaken to our lives as something more than a textbook/cookbook piece of work. He would have us be apprentice cooks, learning our craft directly from the Master Chef.

We do, of course, have a set of instructions—the church's teaching, the rules and directives of Christian tradition. These are our resources, our ready reference. They're the ballpark in which we play, and work, and live. And someone might, without thinking, go so far as to say we have a cookbook—the Bible. But I would resist that analogy. God's Word is a living thing, not ink marks printed on paper between leather covers. We are doing more than merely following a recipe when we approach the Bible as a living Word, in which God speaks today. We are coming into the presence of a Master who, as we listen, offers to take us in hand and instruct us in the ways of culinary artistry.

"Unless your righteousness exceeds that of the scribes and the Pharisees, you will never enter the kingdom of heaven," Jesus says. I really wish he hadn't said that. Because I think we get the wrong idea in our head when we hear the word *righteousness*. "Righteousness"—it's a word that causes a lot of trouble. I get hung up on it. Maybe you do too. Always concerned about doing right. Being right. Making sure that I'm right. Making sure that others know I'm right. Justifying my rightness, no matter how wrong my rightness really is. Comparing my rightness to others' lesser degree of rightness. Or (this is the flip side) getting depressed because others' rightness looks more right than my rightness. All this causes a lot of trouble. It can tie a person in knots. You can finally end up so concerned about being right that you come to love being right more than you love God. And then you are a recipe follower and not a cook.

Dietrich Bonhoeffer wasn't right when, after agonizing struggle, he joined those who were conspiring to assassinate Hitler. There is a law: "Thou shalt do no murder." So he wasn't right. Or was he?

One Lent years ago, there was a "hunger meal" in our parish. It was deliberately set up to dramatize the gulf between the affluent minority and the impoverished majority of our planet. The parishioners who came were arbitrarily assigned to areas of the dining hall. Six were ushered to a large, elegantly set table groaning beneath the weight of succulent dishes. Twelve were put in a humdrum setting with plain but adequate food. Thirty-two were crowded in an ill-lit corner around one creaky card table with a meager dish or two of beans. Everyone was told to stay where they were. Those were the rules.

But after a while Ralph Chilton broke the rules. He got up from the privileged table and started carrying bowls of food to the table of the poor. He departed from the right way in which he had been instructed at the meal's beginning. He broke the rules. Or did he?

We heard from Paul in one of the lessons this morning. Paul had invested lots of energy, kept on trying to be right, trying so hard it nearly drove him crazy, trying so hard he convinced himself that it was the right thing to do to throw other people in prison for being wrong—even kill them. He was so obsessed that he loved being right more than he loved God. And then God opened his eyes. He'd been studying the cookbook, but God showed him the Cook. And Paul testifies to us today: ". . . I decided to know nothing among you except Jesus Christ, and him crucified." Jesus Christ. He had been found by the best religious and political wisdom of the day to be quite in the wrong, and condemned to die for it. Jesus Christ, dying accursed, dying outside the city wall as an unrighteous man—but justified by God who raised him from the dead. Let *him* be your rightness, Paul says. My sermons are not full of rightness, Paul says, they are full of God's power *to make right*—so that your faith may not rest on human rightness, but on the rightness of God.

"Blessed are those who hunger and thirst for righteousness, for they shall be satisfied." Those are words of Jesus from just a few verses above where our reading today began. Isn't it striking that he uses words about food and drink to describe living in God's Kingdom? If you're hungry for God—hungry for the good things of God, hungry for God's right way—then ask God to help you find the right way in this perplexing life we live. God will come to your assistance. God will guide you as you learn to be a cook in the moral life, not just a recipe follower.

"Blessed are those who hunger and thirst for righteousness. They shall be satisfied." God, not rightness, will satisfy them. "Take, eat. This is my body, which is given for you." That's what you need to be right with God. God's cooked up a meal for you at the altar rail today. Enjoy it. And ask God to help you learn to be a cook for others.

R. Bruce Birdsey is rector of St. Philip's Episcopal Church,
Brevard, North Carolina.

SECOND SUNDAY IN LENT

Giving Birth to God

John 3:1–17
C. Denise Yarbrough

HAPPY BIRTHDAY to you! Depending upon your age, those words evoke a sense of delight, eager anticipation, and excitement, visions of presents wrapped in brightly colored paper, cake, ice cream, candles, and parties. Or they provoke a sigh of resignation at the inexorable passage of time that takes its toll on all of us. I've got my mind on birthdays because Robin turns ten this week. I had the unparalleled parental experience of the birthday party sleepover this weekend with all the attendant noise, celebration, and exhaustion!

Over the years, I've noticed that my children's birthdays are special to me for reasons vastly different from those that make these birthdays special to them. They love getting all the presents, being the center of attention, having a party thrown in their honor, blowing out the candles on their cake. For me, their birthdays remind me of two days in my own life that I still remember as if they were yesterday, that changed the course and quality of my life forever.

The experience of giving birth was, without a doubt, one of the most profound spiritual experiences I have ever known. As my children began to move within me early in the pregnancies—as I felt those first flutters that later became agonizing kicks—I was astonished and awed at the mystery of God's creative power, at God's ability to bring life into the world, and at my role as vehicle for that process. Through the months of waiting—the sickness, the exhaustion, the physical transformation that turned my body into something I did not know—I became acutely aware that a power far beyond my limited capacity to comprehend was working toward a purpose I could not define, but to which I could only submit. The birth of a child is one of those defining, liminal experiences, not only for that child and its parents, but also for the entire human family into which the child is born. The birth process is no minor matter.

Jesus and the Pharisee named Nicodemus speak of birth. Jesus tells Nicodemus that "no one can see the kingdom of God without being born from above" (in some translations, the phrase is "born again" or "born anew"). Nicodemus, taking Jesus' words literally, asks how this is possible, since no one can reenter a mother's womb and be born again. Jesus explains that he is referring to a spiritual birth, not a fleshly one.

In his conversation with Nicodemus, Jesus uses the deceptively simple image of birth to describe a complex and lifelong process, what Margaret Guenther describes as "the birth of God in the human soul."[1] Unfortunately the phrase "to be born again" has been so overused in our culture that we may well miss the depth and richness of the experience to which Jesus refers. Spiritual birth, or rebirth, is as profound and life-changing as physical birth. If, as God is being born into our souls, we are attentive to God's signals, and surrender to God's timing, our lives will be transformed as fundamentally and irrevocably as mine was the day my child was born.

Jesus says that we must be "born anew" or "born again/from above" to see the kingdom of God. If we think about what "birth" involves, we can begin to understand the depth and complexity of the metaphor that Jesus chooses to represent the journey of faith. For people of faith, "the birth of God in our soul is our own true birth."[2]

Ten years ago this week, I lay in the birthing room at New York Hospital, enduring the pain of labor, the shedding of blood and tearing of flesh that are part and parcel of bringing new life into the world. Leading up to that momentous day were nine months of anticipation, preparation, physical discomfort, exhaustion and illness. I remember my body feeling as though it had been invaded by an alien. I remember the vulnerability that my unbalanced girth forced upon me. I was unable to climb stairs without feeling as though I'd run the marathon. I couldn't bend over or see my feet. I could barely get out of a chair without a crane. Pregnancy is an exciting time of unexpected and unknown changes, emotional and physical highs and lows, joy mingled with sadness, eager expectancy, and unaccustomed sleepiness. When the time comes for the long awaited birth, the process is messy and painful, both for the mother and for the child. It is also a dangerous process, during which mother, child, or both could die. Even in the midst of the anticipation and joy of the birth event, there is an element of fear and dread, and an uneasy sense of danger lurking in the shadows.

Our spiritual birth, the birth of God in our soul, is a similar process. Like physical birth, it will not necessarily follow a predictable pattern.

Just as some women don't even realize they are pregnant for months, our spiritual rebirth may be starting in us long before we are consciously aware of it. God may well have started the process quietly and mysteriously without our even knowing it until, one day, as we go about our ordinary lives doing ordinary things, we suddenly become aware of God's presence and grace in our lives, and wonder how it is we never saw it before.

On the other hand, just as some women suffer terrible nausea and exhaustion when they become pregnant, for some people the spiritual birthing process begins in the midst of spiritual or emotional upheaval, exhaustion, tension, stress, or pain. Just as the physical and emotional state of a pregnant woman changes through the course of a pregnancy, our emotional and spiritual state may ebb and flow as we are being born in the Spirit, leaving us feeling good, strong, content, and in control one minute, and completely at sixes and sevens the next. As we go through the days of our lives, through periods of calm and periods of transition or stress, our spiritual birth process is proceeding, on God's timetable, to its inexorable end. Spiritual birth may have a long gestation period, perhaps a lifetime. For some, the experience of spiritual birth will come as an overwhelming, easily identifiable "born again" experience, much like St. Paul's conversion on the road to Damascus. For others, it will be a much slower, more subtle process, transforming them into the children God created them to be without their necessarily being aware of the changes, until one day, like the pregnant woman who can no longer ignore the ever increasing size of her belly, they realize that something is going on here, and Someone is at work!

Just as the pregnancy itself has phases and cycles, so, too, does the labor and delivery. We all can go through our lives, living our daily routine, engaging with friends, family, coworkers, making plans, doing our work, going to school, raising our kids, caring for our elderly parents, taking life's ups and downs as they come, much as the pregnant woman learns to deal with the daily variances of her pregnancy. At some point, however, the moment of truth comes. I will never forget the sinking feeling I had at my first Lamaze class, as the instructor began to speak of the mechanics of labor and delivery, when I realized that the only way out of that pregnant state, the only way back to "normal" life, was through the process of labor and delivery. I knew there was no going back, I could only go forward, and what "forward" meant was through the pain and agony of childbirth. What I did not realize then was that it was not possible to return to what had been "normal" life before the pregnancy. After the baby was born, life was changed forever.

For all of us, our spiritual pregnancy will only end with labor and the necessary passage through pain and agony to the process of the birth of ourselves as God intended us to be. And life after that will be forever transformed. Like the process of physical birth, spiritual birth or rebirth is a time of concentration, heightened awareness, and hard work. But also a time of letting go, of surrendering to the purpose God has in mind for us. As a physical labor progresses, it starts with pains that are far apart and manageable with simple breathing exercises. It moves through successively more frequent and more intense pains, and culminates in a phase known as transition, during which time many women believe it would be better to die than to go on. At this point in the process, the mother feels as if she has completely lost control, and that no amount of previous work has adequately prepared her for this reality. Yet just at that point in the labor, when she thinks there is no way it can be survived, the woman is actually on the brink of that long awaited end, the birth of her child.

The same process occurs in spiritual birth. Life always has its ups and downs, which can often be managed and controlled. At some point, however, a major transition occurs. It is often at times of extreme chaos and pain, times of grief or loss due to death, illness, divorce, or loss of employment, times of physical transition, like moving, graduating from school, retiring after many years of working, or facing the empty nest as the last child leaves for college, that we are most likely to experience God being born in our soul. In those chaotic, painful times, as we experience emotional and/or spiritual exhaustion, when we feel forsaken, lonely, and ill prepared for the trial at hand, we may be on the brink of our spiritual birth, and more receptive to God's saving grace than at any other time in our lives.

In the process of being born again spiritually, we participate in the birth process, both as one giving birth and as one being born. As we struggle to survive whatever version of transition we experience, we also emerge from it as a newborn child of God. Through the process of physical birth, that painful, bloody, messy process, a child leaves the darkness, security, quiet, calm and comfort of the womb, and is thrust, usually screaming, into the light, into a world of sights, sounds, and colors, into relationship with others and a life journey to a destination that God will choose. Spiritual birth takes us from the darkness of our own pain or complacency or apathy, into the light of relationship with God and neighbors that may not always be comfortable, nor feel safe, but is certainly rich and colorful.

The spiritual birthing process may not happen only once—it can recur again and again in our journey with God. Until we die, we are always becoming, always moving, always in the process of being born. Even that last earthly transition, our bodily death, is actually a birth into new life. The sickness and suffering that often precede bodily death are like the birth pangs, the labor, that will result in new birth, this time to eternal life.

So when you feel as though things are out of control in your world or your life, remember Jesus' words to Nicodemus about being born in the spirit. Know that you are safe in the hands of the divine midwife, and await with eager anticipation the birth of God in your soul.

C. Denise Yarbrough is rector of the Church of the Transfiguration, Towaco, New Jersey.

---

1. Margaret Guenther, *Holy Listening: The Art of Spiritual Direction* (Boston: Cambridge, 1992), p. 85.

2. See note 1 above.

THIRD SUNDAY OF LENT

Thirsty and Thin

John 4:5–42
Daniel Pearson

"I CAME to this church five years ago as a tourist and ended up a pilgrim." These words are the testimony of a parishioner of Trinity Episcopal Church in Santa Barbara, California. I plucked them from an article by Nora Gallagher that appears in a recent issue of the *Utne Reader*. Its lovely and intriguing title is "The Thin Place Where God Lives." Ms. Gallagher is a long-time Episcopalian, having been baptized in 1965 at age fifteen. Like many "good Episcopalians," however, she dropped out of church at age twenty, and only recently dropped back in. She is both a self-proclaimed baby boomer and a "returnee" to the church of her youth.

What is of interest is why she decided to come back, to be a visitor. It wasn't that the church was so lively. In fact, she reports low attendance, low energy, and low morale. Sadly, even the priest, "a dark haired, middle-aged man," looked depressed. Basically, she concludes, it was "an unhappy place."

But something was there. "Here I am," she writes, "in an empty church. Between the rows of pews, on the tile floor, under the silent cross. I walk along a boundary, a place between heaven and earth. The Celts called it a thin space. . . . Above me, the roof's ribs curve into its spine, an inverted keel. In this church . . . we practice to be thin, to live in space, to go through the narrow door."[1]

As Ms. Gallagher moved in her status from visitor to pilgrim over the years, she increasingly experienced the place as "thin"—a kind of heaven's gate. And the community itself became, for her, transparent of God, as they lit candles for justice, and held vigil for the dying.

What is it, we ask, that draws us more and more into the thin space, the holy place that gets us in touch with God? God, I suppose, entering the world, playing hide and seek. Enticement. Open doors, empty spaces— sacred places. Communities gathered. Wells and water. And Jesus.

"I came to this church five years ago as a tourist and ended up a pilgrim." So said Nora Gallagher in Santa Barbara.

"I came to this well a few hours ago as a servant and ended up a believer."

So might the woman in ancient Samaria have said. For her, the awareness was not "thinness," but thirst. On arrival at the well at Sychar, I'm betting she was more dutiful than thirsty, more programmed for performance than aware of the sacred dimension of her daily routine.

But then she met up with Jesus. He helped her get in touch. Through ordinary conversation he changed the angle of light, helping her see in a new way. In coming to him, she was doing nothing other than what needed to be done: chores, a household task. Was she thirsty? At this point, I doubt it. The point of her routine was to keep her and others from feeling thirst. Be organized. Get water every day so you don't run out. Habits can be helpful.

But they can also foreclose awareness of thinness and thirst. So Jesus brings a surprise: he asks the wrong person—Jews don't ask Samaritans, a real man doesn't talk to a woman—for a drink. He knows she's thick and earthbound, not really aware of things heavenly. He engages the woman in wonderfully confusing and provocative conversation: "If you knew the gift of God, and who it is that is saying to you, 'Give me a drink,' you would have asked him, and he would have given you living water."

Does the woman get the full import of what Jesus is talking about? No. So they talk more about the water. She asks for some. Does she fully understand what she's asking for? No. More engagement. More conversation.

And then Jesus, hard ball out of the blue: "Go, call your husband, and come back." Where did that come from? Talk about changing the subject and putting someone on the spot! Jesus has the goods on her: five husbands, at least. But rather than stomp off and get all offended, she uses this occasion of judgment—the shock of it—as a wedge for new insight: "Sir, I see that you are a prophet."

Slowly, through dialogue, encounter, and engagement, the light is coming through. Through Jesus the rays of heaven are reaching earth and, more importantly, they are coming into her heart—a growing illumination of who Jesus is. Keep going. We've moved from Jesus as merely a thirsty man at the well to a sage proffering living water, to a prophet, to, well, maybe even the Messiah!

And finally, when she joins the chorus of those in her own little village who see for themselves who Jesus is, she nods with approval: This is truly the Savior of the world! The woman who came to the well five hours, five days, five years ago as a servant, finds herself nicely thirsty, hanging around with fellow villagers who spent two days with Jesus. Now everyone is thirsty and "thin."

So what about us—our experience of thinness and thirst? Are we so earthbound that we've lost touch with heaven? Not completely, for sure. That's why we've come here today. Why we make St. Clement's our habit. Here we listen for gospel. As we overhear the conversation between Jesus and the woman at the well, we recollect the work of the Spirit in us to help us see Jesus in a new light. Little by little, we too are getting it: God in the thinness of this Body of Christ. The Spirit of God increasing our thirst for the spiritual, for the living water. We, also, can use Nora Gallagher's words about St. Clement's, this sacred place: "Above me, the roof's ribs curve into its spine, an inverted keel. In this church . . . we practice to be thin, to live in space, to go through the narrow door."

Like the Samaritan woman, we have come to ask, "Give me this water." Like Ms. Gallagher in her church, we have said in this one, "Let's make something happen for God's sake here."

Having a thirst for God and having the experience of the church and the world as "thin" involves getting into the act. We must come to the well not only out of habit, but also in expectation of an encounter with Christ. In our coming to church, we might well consider the old-fashioned idea of being prepared. For most of us this will consist simply of creating a kind of empty space within ourselves, allowing a proper thirst, so that the refreshing word of God may more readily have its effect. We should anticipate engaging Jesus through sacred Scripture and godly play. Having served the needs of others in Christ's name, humbly we offer our labor. We give thanks for God's justice and righteousness. In our prayers for the dying, we stand with them in that narrow place that leads to a greater light.

It is the gift of God revealed in Jesus that inhabits our hearts and awakens our thirst for holy things. And I suppose the intriguing thing about this gift is that it involves not only a strange stirring within us—a draw, a pull, a curiosity, say, about the church—but also *asking*. We go back to the words Jesus spoke to the woman at the well after he surprised her with asking for a drink of water: "If you knew the gift of God, you would have *asked*, and he would have given you living water."

Normally, we don't ask for gifts. We simply receive them. Yet Jesus encourages asking. In doing so, he points to the freedom he wants us to have in our relationship with God. Because it is characterized fundamentally by love, at best, we freely enter in. God may take the initiative to lead us to the well or to awaken a holy thirst within, but our asking, our wanting, our desire, our saying "Yes" adds to the energy of life and love.

Way before the Samaritan woman came to a full understanding of who Jesus was or what she was really up to with Jesus, remember how she asked for water, saying, "Sir, give me this water." In asking God, we testify to our desire to see things "thin" and to be free.

In asking, we receive. That is clearly the testimony of Scripture. The more time the woman at the well spent in dialogue with Jesus, the more enlivened and perceptive she became. Near the story's end we find her not only alive in the possibility of faith for herself, but also running off to testify to others. She runs to the city saying to the people, "Come and see the man who told me everything I have ever done!" Then through her testimony, they are stirred to belief.

The living water of God in us is meant to move. We are not to be a Dead Sea. As we share our faith with others in word and deed, ripples form, even waves occur. All because God acts and is alive in Christ and the church. Jesus invites us to come to the well. He wants us to be in touch with our true thirst, so he can give us living water. As we bend down and drink of his well of life, we find, on looking up, a new light. And in looking to the world, we discover that more and more places are amazingly and wonderfully "thin."

Daniel Pearson is rector of St. Clement's Church,
St. Paul, Minnesota.

---

1. Nora Gallagher, "The Thin Place Where God Lives," *Utne Reader*, iss. 91. Jan./Feb. 1999, pp. 29–31.

THIRD SUNDAY IN LENT

Five Samaritan Husbands

John 4:5–42
Gretchen M. B. Pickeral

SHE WAS weary that day—one of those days when everything seemed to go wrong, from the moment she got up to the moment she realized the water was gone, and she would have to hike up the long hill to Jacob's Well in the heat of the day.

There was nothing for it. Her little goat needed water to provide the minute amounts of milk and cheese that were keeping her alive. Nobody knew about the goat. Thank the mercy of Adonai that she was a quiet one, that little goat. Women were allowed no possessions, but some of her dear friends had brought a goat and bread. When Seth had died, his brother would not take her into his own household, so she had no place to be.

He had been so generous and kind, that old one, Seth. He was alone, the uncle living in his brother's tents and supporting the household. His own losses had made him kind to her. He had waited for three babies to be born, the seeds of the next generation of his family. He had buried each young wife, as their attempts failed to present him with his own child. The lines of loss had been etched deeply in his face, but the loving kindness of Adonai had softened him in his sorrow and grief. His grief had led him to her.

The night her third husband had died she had stepped outside and hunkered against the entrance. She managed to throw her shawl over her head before the wailing scraped up out of her throat, and tumbled out onto the rutted path. It was low and long, and wafted across the dew-laden morning into the village, as the mist rises from damp humus in the crisp air. She wasn't sure she could ever stop.

She cried for the death. She sobbed for the brother she had truly married so many years ago. They had loved each other from the moment their families had introduced them. She had wanted to be everything with him, tender wife, gathering homemaker, generous neighbor, and loving mother. When he died two months later with the sheep, on the mountain, she knew a part of her had died then, too. His brother took her as his second wife, just as the law required, but she was last in line and he was courteously disinterested.

The bad food that struck him and his first wife took some of the children too. The whole household had fallen ill, and when it was over she was left with no husband, no child of her own, and the third brother worried about marriage to a woman who had already buried two men. He knew what the law required, and he was childless. She was grateful for his obedience and his attentions. Perhaps she would finally bear fruit and become completely one of the village women, respected companion and part of the circle of wisdom.

She celebrated the trips to the well then. All the women gathered in the early hours to tell of the night's duties and the evening's exchanges with their haggard mountain men. They talked of problems, joys, and sorrows. Glances sometimes told it all as they stood together at the well. Then, in the evening they would recount the day's adventures and dip their pitchers for the evening meal. Only a small amount would be needed at night; that evening trip to the well was mostly for reassurance. "How did your day go?" "What mercy did Adonai bestow today?" "Did your patience hold as well as Adonai's loving-kindness?" It was a gift just to make the trip sometimes—to have a place to tell her story and listen to the others' managing of their lives.

Sitting outside, at the entrance to their home, she had wept for him and the twisted remains from the trampling stampede. Several men had been tossed and stomped by the panicked animals. When they brought the wounded back, she knew that his injuries were the worst. She could do little more than wash him, and ask for blessings on his ebbing breath.

She wept for the loss of her household, her place. She wept for the womb still empty. It meant there would be no place for her to fit. No part of the village would dare to take in a woman who had let three husbands die while she remained barren. She would surely be branded now, if only from ignorance and fear.

Then there had been the miracle of Seth. What woman could ever hope for a fourth man to take her in? He had stepped gently up to her that night, the lines of his own triple grief carved over his visage. These mountain men never wept, for they lived with loss and uncertainty. But that night the glistening tracks of sorrow sparkled down either side of his sunburned nose and disappeared into the thick of his beard. He stared straight into her face and told her he would help her bury this third man, his cousin. He told her she would come to live with him, and they would sit *shiva* together for their losses. He told her he would wait for her grief, and she would wait for his. He was old, and had no need for children; Adonai would surround them for their years and give them strength and courage to go on.

Now he was dead, too. Just dead. A year had passed. They had kept good and quiet company, and as they both prepared to lay their cloaks of mourning down, he died one night, quietly, in his sleeping. She went to him from her pallet in the morning, on the way to the deep cool waters of the village well, and found him still and cold.

And so she was numb by now, this weary, hot day. Only two months had passed since she had found her fourth husband dead on his sleeping pallet. His brother would not take her in. The law expected this, protection for the widows. The childless widow must be taken as wife by the remaining brother so the seed might live on in the next generation. By the law this brother was her fifth husband. His fear had made him refuse. She couldn't blame him.

She slept in the brambles at the edge of the village. The goat kept her warm. Abby had secreted it to her, just as its suckling kid had begun to wean. Iscah brought her grains and breads from the scraps at her home after sundown each night, missing only the evening of Shabbat. The women couldn't speak to her or openly befriend her. Perhaps she would live as an outcast all her life. Perhaps she would starve, or freeze when the snows came.

The elders had met twice now to render a decision, but had not been able to agree. So her heart was heavy as she climbed the hill, her thoughts were still and dull to reason. Only Adonai could give her hope, and even her prayers had run dry these last weeks. In many ways it was just simpler to climb to the well at the heat of midday. None of the women would see her or meet her then. She wouldn't have to bear up under their pitying stares. She wouldn't have to long for the kind words that she knew they wanted to speak, but could not.

Now, what was this? A group of filthy, foreign travelers gathered around the sacred well of Jacob. What were they up to? Where had they come from? Good, they were moving from the rocky edge of the crystalline, burbling wellspring. She was in no shape to be polite or deferential to a band of gawking strangers from Jerusalem. She could tell that they were citified by their tunics, staffs, and sandals. No mountain men, these.

Oh, dread! One of them was resting on the edge, while the others moved off. She would keep her head down, dip her pitcher, and move away fast. Her heart ached and her mind was blank. She wanted no trouble or interference.

As she approached, this Jewish stranger spoke. What a nuisance! What a scandal! Perhaps she should never have come here alone. Who would protect her? Who would know if she was attacked? Her broken heart pounded in her chest. She couldn't tell if she was more afraid or angry. He asked for water. She couldn't stop herself.

"How do you speak to me, you a *Judean*? How can a *Judean* man ask a woman, a woman from Samaria, for a drink of water?" She kept her eyes down, her voice as even as her trembling chest would permit.

He turned to face her more directly and she braced herself. Would he strike her for speaking? Would he grab her and force her to entertain his friends? His voice was firm and strong. "If you knew the gift of Adonai, and if you knew who was asking 'Give me a drink,' you would have asked him and he would give you the water of life."

Now he was telling her riddles; and he had no pitcher or cup hanging from his girdle. How would he provide water to her? He was taunting her. This was going to be bad. He was a mean one. "You have no vessel, sir." Still lowering her face and eyes to the dirt, "From where will you fetch this water of life? Jacob gave our ancestors this deep and cool, clear well. Adonai gave it for his sons and flocks, and it is ours by rights. Are you greater than this?"

His answer came without hesitation. "All who drink here must return again. Those who drink the water of life that I give will never thirst. The water I will give will become a wellspring within them gushing up life eternal."

The sorrow in her heart seemed to bear her downwards. She was nearly tumbling to her knees as she stammered, "Give me this water of life so I might not thirst, spare me from this daily trip to draw from the well."

He seemed to hear the fear in her voice then. He reached kindly to steady her as her knees threatened to buckle, but she drew away. She knew he mustn't touch her; he knew it, too. "Go," he offered gently, "find your husband and return with him." He was not going to harm her. He was a teacher. He wanted only to help.

She looked up then. She knew she was forbidden to gaze into the face of a man not her husband, a foreign man, not even a villager. "I have no husband," she admitted frankly.

Their eyes met, and froze in time and space. Nothing was there, just his face, his eyes, his kindness and insight. The realization washed over both of them simultaneously. He was looking in to her. He saw her heart and the agony of her grief and loss. He read her every hope and dream and desire to be a woman, wife, and mother. He must have heard the dull ache of her worry, her hunger, the growling of her stomach and the longing of her thirst.

"You are right," he agreed. "You say you have no husband. But you have had five husbands, and the one you have now is not your husband, that is true."

She couldn't move. She couldn't breath. Her gaze met his, and her heart bubbled and burbled like a spring. She thought it would come up from the depths of her soul and fly into the gentle mountain wind.

She gaped and told him: "You speak the truth. You are a seer, a prophet. Tell us where we are to worship then, in the temple at Jerusalem or at the mountain altar of the north?" She knew it was *the* question, the one the rabbis quarreled about, the question that kept Judeans and Samaritans apart. His answer was strange to her but at the same time completely satisfying.

"Neither, woman," he explained. "Whether known or unknown, the age has come for true worship of Adonai to be in breath/wind/spirit—and in truth. God is breath/wind/spirit and worshippers must worship in breath/wind/spirit—and in truth."

"I know," she said, "the savior is coming—the one called 'anointed,' and he will be the messenger of all things."

He met her gaze. He didn't flinch. They could both hear his traveling companions approaching. He smiled and confessed: "I am that one—the one to whom you are speaking now."

The voices were behind her, and she left the pitcher there on the edge of the well. Turning, she elbowed through the group of dusty travelers. They parted politely. She could tell they didn't approve of her speaking with their friend. She didn't care.

She ran. She could barely feel her feet on the steep, rutted trail. She had to tell the others—she had met someone. Someone who knew her, who knew everything about her, and yet still gave her the water of life. He gave it freely; and it had mended her and burst her open like a blossom in the spring rain. She flew into Abby's cooking area and fairly shouted the news to all of Abby's household—could this be the One? The One with the Good Message of God's truth? Then on to Iscah's house, and then to Seth's grieving brother.

She didn't remember her sense of loss and shame in the village. She didn't care. She didn't know her name would be lost in the story. She didn't care. She didn't know this stranger's visit to her village, the words he spoke to her, a thirsty, brokenhearted woman from Samaria, would change her life. But it did. She didn't know his stop in the northern mountains for instruction and guidance would change the village forever. But it did.

She didn't know that what he taught his followers that week by stopping, speaking, and accepting the reapers and sowers together would change the world forever. But he did. And it did.

Gretchen M. B. Pickeral is a conference leader and
consultant in healing and spiritual direction
living in St. Louis, Missouri.

Will I?

John 11:18–44
George Chapman

WHEN I saw that today's Gospel selection recounted the raising of Lazarus, I was pleased. After all, I had just finished writing a reflection piece for the newsletter about resurrection. That which appears to be the primary thrust of the event—and certainly the interpretation given by most preachers most of the time (myself included)—is that Jesus, in raising Lazarus from the dead, did a wonderful thing for all concerned. And how can you argue with that?

As the story opens, the sisters of Lazarus, Martha and Mary, are weeping over their loss. And those who have come to provide the consolation of sitting *shiva* with them are not in much better shape. Even Jesus himself, confronted with the grief-stricken sisters who have literally thrown themselves at his feet, gets caught up in the emotion of the moment, and weeps.

Here is a man, Lazarus, wrenched from his family in what appears to be the prime of life. His sisters, convulsed with grief, both confront (perhaps even chastise) Jesus with the words: "If you had been here, my brother would not have died." Their faith in Jesus as a healer is clear and certain; but the healer has not arrived in time, and the man who lingered several days in his sickness has finally succumbed.

Most of us are familiar with serious illness, and with the death of a loved one. Many of us can feel with Mary and Martha not only the grief, but also the frustration. Perhaps something more might have been done; but it was not done in time. The worst has happened. The patient has died. The family is devastated.

But the story of the life of Lazarus has not been fully told. Jesus, after absorbing the grief of his friends, after joining in the weeping, after challenging Martha's faith, after offering up a prayer to God, cries with a loud voice: "Lazarus! Come out!" And . . . out of the tomb he comes.

So, what can we say about that? The tears of mourning are, presumably, turned to tears of joy. Tragedy becomes triumph. Death is turned back. Lazarus rejoins his family and friends. Another job by Jesus well done!

Is that how we understand this remarkable episode: as a sort of success story for Jesus, and a lucky break for Lazarus? That is not how John, the Gospel writer, sees it. That is not what John finds most important for his purposes.

You see, John's Gospel has a kind of internal pattern or movement, the design of which is to set out a succession of signs (in the form of miracles) that increase in power and marvel, from the changing of water into wine at the wedding feast in Cana (the first sign), through the healing of the blind, culminating in the raising of Lazarus from the dead. And to what do these signs point? To Jesus as the Messiah. That is John's aim. Lazarus, dead and then raised to life, is but a pawn of sorts. It could have been anyone. The purpose is not to do a favor for a friend (though how nice that is how things worked out), but to prove in a most impressive and indisputable fashion that Jesus is the Christ of God.

As dramatic as they are, then, the most important words Jesus speaks in this whole episode are not "Lazarus! Come out!" but rather "Whoever believes in me, though they die, yet shall they live." And good for us that this is the case! Good for us: Because, while this is a story about other people who live long ago and far away, it also involves us. For we can be confident that our faith will be tested by death—the death of someone we love, or death in a situation that shocks and dismays us.

Deep down, in a most personal manner, I know that the story of the raising of Lazarus is about me. I am in it, playing most of the parts, save one. When someone dies whom I dearly love, especially if that death seems untimely, the pain of my grief makes me into Mary and Martha. I have the words of Martha, to be sure: "I know that he will rise again in the resurrection. . . . I believe that you are the Christ." But I also have Mary's accusation: "If you had been here he would not have died." Faith and bereavement enmeshed; anger, pain, and hope rolled into one. My feelings about God, like Martha's feelings about Jesus, are at best confused and ambivalent.

At other times I am a bystander. I was not close to the one who has died; my role is as a comforter. Or I observe from afar a tragedy—the death of a child at the hands of a drunk driver, a natural disaster, the cruel death of the innocent in a terrorist attack or civil war. I do whatever I can to help those left behind. I care. And I wonder, "Why did this have to happen? Could not he who opened the eyes of the blind man have kept them from dying?"

And sometimes, in my grief, I am also like Lazarus: bound, entombed. My aversion to death binds me; my desire to be with loved ones, now lost, is powerful, immediate, and tinged with doubt that I will be reunited with them in God's time. I want to be with them, and I want it now. You might even say that at such moments of grief and doubt, pain and uncertainty, I am dead to the world. I am shut up alone in a tomb— a tomb that keeps out light and life, joy and community.

Bound. Entombed. Alone. And out there—Jesus. He knows. He understands. He cares. He loves. He weeps. And he cries with a loud voice: "Come out!"

Will I?

George M. Chapman is rector of St. Paul's Church, Brookline, Massachusetts.

PALM SUNDAY

Blood

Matthew 27:1–54
Joyce Scherer-Hoock

".... [T]HIS IS my blood of the covenant, which is poured out for many for the forgiveness of sins. . . ."

"When Judas, his betrayer saw that Jesus was condemned he repented . . . saying, 'I have sinned in betraying innocent blood.'"

"So when Pilate saw that he was gaining nothing, but rather that a riot was beginning, he took water and washed his hands . . . saying, 'I am innocent of this man's blood, see to it yourselves.' And all the people answered, 'His blood be on us and our children!'"

Blood.

Human beings grow in blood. We are born out of blood, and in it. All our lives, it flows through our veins. We die from its loss. Blood is the carrier of life and death. Scientifically, blood is a fluid—mostly water, but containing the complex elements that allow the body to breath, and to nourish and repair itself. In the blood, sickness is combated, waste carried away. Blood has many meanings to us. We treat blood as precious: banking it, analyzing it, transfusing it. We treat it as filthy: In the hospital, it is disposed of as hazardous waste. The monthly bleeding of women is unmentionable. The type of blood we have can tell us who we belong to—who our father or mother was, or wasn't. In our blood is our connection to the whole human race. Passed down in the womb. Mother to child. Mother to child. Mother to child.

In the Old Testament, life is connected to *blood*. The word blood could stand for the bare life of a human being. When Cain kills Abel, his brother, Abel's blood is spoken of as crying out to God from the ground. The kosher law for the Jew reflects a profound respect for blood. Human beings are entitled only to the meat of an animal that comes from the earth and returns to the earth, while life, the blood, belongs to Yahweh, to God alone.

Blood.

Blood is at the heart of Christianity also, though it may be hard for us as modern, rational, polite and antiseptically inclined people to admit. Funny, isn't it, how, as we have become increasingly embarrassed to talk about blood in church—television and movie screens are increasingly bathed in blood.

This morning we retold the story that stands at the heart of Christianity. Read it. Acted it out. From the hosannas of the excited crowd at the triumphal entry, to the stone at the door of the tomb. But at the center, the heart, of that story stands just one person. Bruised. Bleeding. Jesus the Galilean. Jesus of Nazareth. And his blood. His life's blood poured out.

What do you make of his blood?

"His blood be on us and our children!" cries the crowd. Are they an insane, bloodthirsty mob? Death is the penalty for blasphemy. According to Levitical law, the blasphemer is to be put to death by the whole community. Are they just doing what they think is right? The crowd, interestingly, accepts responsibility, while all others—the religious leaders, Herod, Pilate—attempt to avoid it. And though this passage has been used by Christians to persecute Jews—to call them "Christ killers"—the dramatic reading does right when it puts those words in our mouths—yours and mine—when we become the crowd. "His blood be on US and on our children."

Our modern, Western, rational minds struggle with the limits of responsibility. We like to think that the only responsibility we have is for the things that we, specifically and individually, do. Our little "s" sins. Which, of course, are minor, not important, really, in the great scheme of things. They don't hurt anyone. We only do what we need to do. No big deal.

But deep inside, we know better. We know that we are all connected. As a proverb says, "The movement of the wings of a butterfly sends out ripples that can produce a typhoon a world away." In the Global Village, and with developing ecological understanding, we are learning once again what the ancients knew: that all human beings are connected in a deep, organic way. That the waste produced in Manhattan can affect people living in North Dakota. That the chemicals used to clean machinery at a plant, dumped on land in Woburn, can lead to the sickness and death of children born years later, living miles away. That the sweatshirt with the name of a college on it, worn by a teen here in America was made in Asia by a child, paid a few cents a day, who will never have an opportunity to learn to read or write. That the toy my child gets at McDonald's was made by a person whose protest for democracy placed him in a Chinese prison, where there is little to eat, and no meal is happy. We *are* connected to people and places far away, and responsible to and for them.

Last week, we spoke of the mass graves of the twentieth century in Germany and Poland, in Armenia, El Salvador, Cambodia, and now Kosovo. Who is responsible for those graves? For that blood? If we can say we are not responsible for this one, what about the other? I wonder how a German SS officer could sing "Silent Night" and kiss his child on Christmas Eve, yet participate in gassing Jews. But my own father came home and kissed me after standing ready to bomb Cuba during the missile crisis.

Who among us is wholly innocent? Just by living and participating in an economic and political system we participate in its wrongs as well as its rights. We participate in Sin—with a big "S". The Sin of the world. Attempts to wash our hands of responsibility, like Pilate did, are only partially convincing—even to us.

A friend of mine is an Episcopal priest. In spite of or perhaps because of his seminary education, he was a skeptic and a thorough-going rationalist. In seminary, he told me, he and his friends would sit around and make fun of the Nicene Creed. They couldn't believe that anybody would believe anything so primitive. So absurd. So superstitious.

Then one day he was persuaded to sit with a group of people who were praying; and they began to pray for him. Nothing happened. He got bored. They continued. He tried to think of a polite way to leave.

Then, inexplicably, he was caught up in a strange vision; he saw a canvas, an artist's canvas. It was big, bigger than any real canvas could be. It stretched to the horizon. And it was covered with red. At first he thought it was paint. Then he realized it was blood. Red, red blood that ran, and dripped down toward the bottom of the canvas. Down to an umbilical cord that was connected to his mother, then to his father, and then to the entire German race, and to him. And it dripped blood. He was overcome with guilt and began to cry and pound his leg. "I felt the guilt of the German people for the holocaust," he said. He was born in 1948. But *he felt his connection* to that crime; and he pounded his leg and wept.

But then, he said, while he was crying, something changed. He realized that the red paint on the canvas, the blood, wasn't just the blood of the German race, or the Jewish people they had killed; it was also the blood of Jesus.

He has never had a second vision, but that one changed his life. He is a different person, because the blood of Jesus means something different to him. It is no longer a primitive, superstitious religious relic, but a profound and passionate inward knowing of his connection both to guilt and to redemption. The blood of Jesus means something different to him.

What do you make of the mystery of the blood of Jesus? We can either ignore and deny our connection to blood, and the blood-guiltiness of our race, to our visceral connection with the whole race—in all its glory, and all its horror. We can deny what we know inside. Turn the music up a little louder. Surround ourselves with more and more distraction. And then wonder why silence scares us, and why our children despair.

Or, we can take the plunge, and put our trust in the blood of Jesus, which, Scripture tells us, "cleanses us from every sin." We can put our whole trust in Christ's grace and love. In God's mercy and forgiveness—because who, other than God, can forgive the human race? Who else can make whole our unwholeness? Restore the unholy mess we have made of creation?

Do I understand how this works? Can I explain it? No, I can't. I can only witness to the fact, as my friend did, that when I embrace the blood of Jesus, and accept that its shedding was on my behalf and has power for me, my life is different. It changes qualitatively. And the more I learn to lean into a wholehearted trust in Jesus' blood, applying it to every wound, error, failure, and sorrow of my life, the more I find in it a source of healing, truth, and joy.

What do you make of the blood of Jesus? What might the blood of Jesus make of you? Thanks be to God for the blood of Jesus.

Joyce Scherer-Hoock is associate rector of Trinity Church, Tropsfield, Massachusetts.

PALM SUNDAY

A Passionate People

Matthew 21:1–11; 27:1–54
Jamie Lynn Hamilton

WE BEGAN the service this morning with shouts of joy, praising Jesus Christ as the King that cometh in the name of the Lord. The church is filled with palms and, like that first crowd so long ago, we celebrated the triumphant entry of Jesus into Jerusalem. We joined with their voices, their dances, their enthusiastic cries: "Hosanna to the Son of David."

If we could only stop there! But the liturgy of Palm Sunday never lets us sit with that glory for very long. Soon we move out of celebration into betrayal. Out of life, into death. In a dramatic turn, as the crowd who first acclaimed Jesus as God's son, we have now asked Pilate to crucify him. The more Pilate protests, the louder we shout, "Let him be crucified!" Instead of branches carried in his honor, we strip another tree to become the instrument of his death. We tell Pilate that we want an execution, and we are willing to accept our role as executioner.

What happened? What went wrong? How can we, one minute, be a people exhibiting signs of faith and the next minute be willing to bury that faith along with the man who is our hope and belief? Our cries have not only turned against Jesus but have turned upon ourselves. We have just ordered the death of God and are willing to accept the consequences. We are a doomed people, the death of our God on our hands. Alone and alienated from ourselves and our world, soon there will be nothing for us to do but cry into the night.

In telling the story of our cries of "Hosanna!" and our cries of "Crucify!" Matthew uses the same Greek verb, *krazo*, which means to cry out with a guttural sound. The word is like croak, and it is based on the croaking sound of ravens to suggest a rough and raucous sound. Outside of the New Testament, this word *krazo* has religious significance in the sphere of the demonic. It is used to describe the voice of the witch, "which is like the bellowing of hounds, the howling of wolves, the hissing of snakes."[1]

It is not the witch, but the demon in the witch who cries out. It is not the men, but the demons in the men that cry out to Jesus, and it is those demons that Jesus drives away. When the disciples see Jesus walking toward them on the sea, and they think he is a ghost, they cry out for fear, using this croaking voice.

Matthew makes it clear. It is the demon within us that makes us cry out, "Crucify him!" But could Matthew be suggesting that it is also the demon within us who cries out, "Hosanna to the Son of David?" Now, this is a much more disturbing thought! Accepting the reality of evil in the face of evil is much more straightforward. Of course, demanding the death of an innocent man is evil. We are prepared to accept this. It is not a shock.

But to accept that there is evil with our good intentions? This is much more difficult. It brings up an assortment of fears and questions. How well do we know ourselves? Can we trust our intentions? Do we have control over our selfish desires, or are we just kidding ourselves? Can we believe that our desires will lead us to God's will for our lives? When we gather together, do we just become a mob, or can we form loving community?

If Matthew is implying that evil was lurking behind our shouts of "Hosanna!" as Jesus entered into Jerusalem, then I think we have to be willing to ask ourselves, "Who are we, anyway? Are we capable of truly becoming the people God wants us to be?"

Matthew's answer is "No." We will not be able to become what God planned for our lives if we are not willing to accept God on God's terms. If we think we can always hold out, at least a little bit, and control God, even if only a smidgen, we will always fall short of God's dream for our lives. Isn't that what the cries of "Hosanna!" are all about? When we throw down our cloaks to give Jesus a royal greeting, we see Jesus as our King, as our Ruler of the Universe, not because he truly is King, but because he will make our lives better, safer, more productive. He will make us kings. He will identify our enemies and crush them. He has come in the name of the Lord to do what we think best. At this point in the Gospel story, we have rejected Jesus' death and suffering. Defining God on our terms is the demon within us that takes control. Jesus enters into Jerusalem, but he isn't really entering into our own lives. Is not this the point of the story? That our own lives are the city of which Jesus wishes to be King. There are many gates Jesus could enter; which he plans to use, we will never know. But when Jesus enters through any one of these gates, he is claiming to be Lord in the city of our lives.[2]

But we don't want God to be who God will be in our lives. We want God on our own terms, and if we can't have God on our own terms, we will cry out, "Crucify him!"

Why do we do this? Why do we want to control God anyway? What are we afraid of? I think it comes down to one simple but profound act—entering into our own paschal mystery.

But we put up our hands. NO, we do not want to suffer, nor do we want to enter into anyone else's suffering. We want to claim Jesus Christ as King in our lives, but not as the Suffering Servant.

And yet, Jesus only comes to us as a suffering servant. As a people of faith, Jesus claims us, and in that claim, we must enter into not only Jesus' suffering, but our own and others'.

Palm Sunday teaches us that suffering is a part of our lives. The simple act of believing in a God who will be who God is, rather than in someone we want God to be, is an opening of ourselves to suffering.

Remember Simon, the man from Cyrene, who found himself bearing the cross for Jesus? He never meant to be there. He did not even know what he was doing. He was pressed into duty, and yet he carried the cross for Jesus.

We, too, can carry each other's crosses. Sometimes we won't even *know* that we are bearing the cross of another. And yet, we *will* be pressed into duty.

I remember a time when I was an unwitting cross bearer. We were living in New York. I was teaching an introductory Bible course to high school seniors—a class no one wanted to teach, and no one wanted to take. I was new on the faculty, so it was mine to tackle. It was a hot September afternoon. School had only been in session a couple of weeks. It was near the end of the day. My voice was tired, I was feeling drained. I didn't know my students very well. The air conditioning wasn't working. I was writing some notes on the board about Abraham and Sarah and the birth of their son, Isaac, when the students started to give me a bad time.

"You don't really believe this stuff, do you, Ms. Hamilton? My God, they were over ninety years old! Yeah, right, they had a kid! What a stupid miracle, anyway! Who cares? Just two tired people in a tired desert."

I tried to ignore their comments, but I could tell they were getting to me. Like the rough and raucous cry of the witch, their questions felt like fingernails running down my chalkboard. How much of this did I believe in, anyway? How did I understand the Bible in terms of my own faith? I thought to myself, "No wonder no one wants to teach this class. What was I thinking of to expose my faith to a bunch of smart adolescents?" I kept on writing. Finally, a student asked me, "Do you believe in miracles, Ms. Hamilton?"

"Yes, I do," I answered, with my back still to the class as I continued to write on the board.

"How can you believe in miracles?"

"Anyone who has worked as a chaplain on the burn unit at New York Hospital, as I have, has seen miracles." The room was silent. I was relieved. But then, I realized that it was too quiet. I turned around and faced the class for the first time that day. "What's up? Something just happened?"

And then a student who hardly had spoken a word in class for two weeks said, "I have been burned. I lived on that burn unit for nine months."

For the first time, I realized he was the only one in the room with a long-sleeve shirt on. "Nine months. You were burned badly."

"Yes, most of my chest, and arms and thighs. I was caught in an explosion on the street."

"God! You have been through hell, and back again! May I see the work done on your arm?" With that he began to roll up his sleeve. We talked about the grafts, and the pain, and the nurses, and his surgeon, Dr. Madden, who was also called Dr. God. While we talked, I ran my hand over his arm admiring how well his body had recovered and the beautiful work done by his surgeon. The bell rang, and our conversation ended.

The next day in the hallway, I ran into the student's mother. She introduced herself and said, "My son has never talked about his burns with anyone. He has kept so much within himself. And last night he told me what happened in your class. It meant so much to him that you touched his burns, and that you were not repelled by them. For the first time, he told me about how he felt, and we talked late into the night about the whole ordeal we had been through. Believe me, it's a miracle." And with that she began to cry.

"You have been keeping a lot in, too," I said. And with that I began to cry, because, of course, I had been keeping a lot in, too. And so we stood in that hallway crying.

The student, the mother, and I were bearing each other's crosses; and through that, we were witnessing God's healing power.

During our lives there are times that we will be able to bear someone else's cross, and help bring them closer to their salvation and to God. And there will be times when *others* bear *our* cross, and bring *us* closer to what God wants for us. All of this is possible because first Jesus bore all our crosses and brought salvation to the world. Because of his wounds, he is not repelled by ours. And he will touch them, admire them, and love them to glory.

On this Palm Sunday, let us claim that our cries of "Hosanna!" are cries of love to a God we know we cannot control. That we are rejoicing with Jesus, as he enters into Jerusalem, because we know that, through the miracle of his resurrection, he has entered into our own lives.

Palm Sunday engages us in a journey, a journey in which we cross over to God. In this journey, we give ourselves back to God, coming to believe that we are a passionate people in love with a passionate God.

Jamie Lynn Hamilton is chair of the Religion Department at Phillips Exeter Academy, Exeter, New Hampshire.

---

1. *Theological Dictionary of the New Testament,* vol. III, ed. Gerhard Kittel (Grand Rapids, Mich.: WM.B. Eerdmans Publishing Company, 1965), 898.

2. Herbert O'Driscoll, *A Time for Good News: Reflections on the Gospel for People on the Go,* Year A (Toronto, Canada: Anglican Book Centre, 1990), 54.

MAUNDAY THURSDAY

Do This in Remembrance of Me

1 Corinthians 11:23–26; Luke 22:14–30
J. Donald Waring

IT IS Day Five of parenthood for Stacie and me, and we are catching on in a hurry to the ins and outs of caring for James Soule Waring. The bags under our eyes should show for all the nursing, burping, diapering, and rocking that goes on round the clock in our home. These are but a few of the outward and visible tasks of parenting, and we wouldn't have it any other way.

Tonight I want to tell you about a deeply personal, inward, and spiritual task of parenting that I hope in some way, someday, to undertake with my son. As the years increase, it will be my challenge to introduce James Soule Waring to James Henry Waring, his grandfather, who died three years ago. Stacie and I pray that little James will have a long and happy relationship with his three surviving grandparents (and a step-great-grandmother), and that each will impress on him the special gifts of his or her personality. But a great sadness for me is that James will not have that opportunity with my father. My son will never in this life meet my father face-to-face. James will never directly experience his grandfather's unflagging positive spirit, or the warm strength of his personality and presence. He will never hear first-hand the familiar sound of my father's voice, speaking yet one more piece of unsolicited advice. My son and my father will never play catch, shoot baskets, or do the things that little boys and their grandfathers do together. Even so, my hope is that James Soule Waring will, in some sense, come to know James Henry Waring—not just know *about* him, but really *know* him. I want to pass on to my son a living remembrance of my father. How will I do it? For me, that will be one of the many inward and spiritual tasks of parenting.

Today is Maundy Thursday, the day in Holy Week that Jesus *began* with friends and life intact, but *ended* utterly deserted. On this evening, everyone around Jesus conveniently forgot the relationship that they had with him. In the Gospel of Luke we have heard how Judas forgot. All it took to strip Judas's memory was thirty pieces of silver, offered as payment to betray Jesus into the hands of those who wanted to kill him. We have heard how the other disciples also forgot. As they ate the Passover meal with Jesus—as Jesus broke the bread and passed the cup, and commanded the disciples to do the same in remembrance of him—the disciples were bickering as to which of them was to be regarded as the greatest. A few hours later, Peter would three times deny any relationship with Jesus. And what of the crowds who the next morning would call out for Jesus' crucifixion? Apparently they forgot that only five days earlier they had spread palm branches in Jesus' path as he entered the city, and cried "Hosanna! Blessed is the King who comes in the name of the Lord!"

So it was that, on the night before he died for us, the people around Jesus all forgot. They forgot his ministry and mission; they forgot his miracles and meals. The stripping of the altar that will end our service tonight dramatizes the stripping of memory, and the emptiness, desertion, and betrayal that resulted.

But that first Maundy Thursday wasn't the end of the forgetting. Not too many years later, the Corinthians also seemed to forget. This new congregation of Christians that had come into being for the sole purpose of following and worshipping Jesus had devolved into a quarreling cluster of factions. Apparently one of these groups would arrive early for the Eucharist and help themselves to the wine before the others could have any. They forgot their focus, which was Jesus Christ. And that was a problem, because their mission included bringing the world around them into a saving relationship with Jesus. How were they going to pass that relationship on to others if they themselves had forgotten? How were they going to communicate a living remembrance of Jesus to people who had never met him face-to-face?

This brings me back to my newborn son. How will I help James to remember a grandfather he will never meet? As the years increase, how will I myself remember? Let me tell you about something that has helped me to remember.

Thirteen years ago when I went off to seminary in New York City, my father committed himself to the extravagant goal of writing one hundred letters to me while I was there. For the next three years he poured himself into those letters. They were not long; some he dashed off while waiting for appointments to begin, or before leaving his office for the day, or while sitting on an airplane waiting for takeoff. They were full of advice, words of unqualified support, and his personal views on everything from biblical authority to the 1986 New York Mets' World Series victory. By the time I graduated from seminary my father had not reached his goal of one hundred letters, but he had written fifty-six.

One of the better things I have done in my life was to save every one of those letters. They remain as something outward and visible. The paper they were written upon, and the ink they were written with, are very much a part of this material reality. I can still read them, and I do. Yet these fifty-six pieces of common note paper, full of scrawled handwriting, are much more than their outward and visible appearance.

When I read them, they communicate an inward and spiritual relationship that continues. They impart something of my father's life, presence, and personality to me. Each one is a personal pep talk. Some of the words he wrote have a profound timelessness about them, speaking to me today with shades of meaning that perhaps I missed years ago. So these letters represent far more than a nostalgic trip down memory lane, dripping with sentimentality. For me they are continually contemporary. Some day, I trust, James Soule Waring and James Donald Waring are going to spend a lot of time together reading these letters, remembering James Henry Waring.

Those letters, and their capacity to convey the presence of a person we cannot see, are a parable for tonight. Tonight, and every night, the person whose presence it is most important for us to remember is Jesus. The person that James Soule, and James Donald, Judas Iscariot, and Simon Peter, and you and yours most need to know is Jesus. Not just know *about* him, but *know him*. How will his living presence be passed on to us?

On this night, even as his closest friends were falling away and forgetting, Jesus left them and us with an outward and visible sign that would forevermore impart his inward and spiritual grace. This is the night that Jesus instituted the Sacrament of his Body and Blood, available to us in common bread and wine. As Luke tells us, Jesus took bread, and when he had given thanks he broke it and gave it to them, saying, "This is my body, which is given for you. Do this in remembrance of me." After supper he took the cup, saying, "This cup which is poured out for you is the new covenant in my blood."

To be sure, the bread and wine are common, earthy substances. We can taste them, touch them, see them. Yet the bread and wine are much more than their appearance. It takes the eyes of faith to see his handwriting and signature upon them. The broken bread is his broken body. The wine poured out is his blood that will be spilled. The bread and wine are his life given for us—his love letter written to us. Within this sign is the presence of Jesus.

Some may ask: how can Jesus possibly be present in common bread and wine? Many great minds and faithful hearts have written volumes to address this concern. But ultimately, the answer is a mystery. We can speak to the question with parables and metaphors: Jesus present in the bread and wine given to us is something like my father present in paper and ink written to me. Each is an outward and visible sign of an inward and spiritual grace. It is like that, and larger than that.

It may come as a relief to you to know that Jesus never said, "Understand this in remembrance of me." He merely said, "Do this in remembrance of me." Comprehension is not necessary to receive the presence of Jesus. Participation is all it takes to awaken to the living memory of Christ. "Do this in remembrance of me." Break the bread and pass the cup in remembrance of Jesus.

Hear again the words of tonight's Epistle: "For I received from the Lord what I also delivered to you, that the Lord Jesus on the night when he was betrayed took bread, and when he had given thanks, he broke it, and said, 'This is my body which is for you. Do this in remembrance of me.'" That's what the Apostle Paul told the Corinthian congregation to do when they were forgetting who and whose they were. That's what you and I do Sunday after Sunday to remember and receive the living presence of Jesus. That's what you and I who are the Church do to pass on to the world a saving relationship with Jesus Christ.

He is forever contemporary. He is here at this Eucharist. He is present in this bread and wine. And we are his guests at this most sacred banquet.

J. Donald Waring is rector of St. Thomas's Church,
Terrace Park, Ohio.

GOOD FRIDAY

Foolishness

John 18:1–19:37
Stephen J. S. Smith

GOOD FRIDAY'S date changes from year to year. April 1, I believe, is the most appropriate date for Good Friday, or at least today's date, the day after All Fools' Day. If the cross is about anything, it is about foolishness. For some, it is foolish to call this Friday "good." What is so good about death by crucifixion? Others can think of the cross as an act of wicked foolishness: the sadistic sacrifice of a son by his supposedly loving father.

But these acts of seeming foolishness, set in context, make a certain sense. The opening verses of John's Gospel tell us that the Word made flesh in Jesus Christ was with God at the beginning of creation. The Word was God. The Word became flesh, and dwelt amongst us. So the cross is not a sadistic sacrifice of a son by his father. The father and the son are one God from the beginning of creation. Christ's death on the cross was, in fact, the death of God Godself.

In this holy knowledge we understand the seeming foolishness of calling this day "good." For the word *good* is a corruption of the early English word *God*. Today, truly, is God Friday.

Even so, a God is supposed to act like a God: "In royal and regal state to reign." A God dying on a cross still seems foolish. Yet Paul tells the Corinthians that, "God's foolishness is wiser than human wisdom." And remember Jesus' warning that we are not to call each other "fool." Maybe, just maybe, he was warning us that *fool* is a sacred word, to be applied only to God.

But what does this act of divine foolishness mean? What lies behind the cross? Behind the scenes, what's going on for God?

We can dare to approach some understanding of the mystery of the cross by looking at God's foolishness in all-too-human terms: the foolishness of lovers. Think of Romeo and Juliet, that sublime story of human love in all its glorious foolishness. The risks they took, the rebellion against their family traditions, the misunderstandings, the tragedy, all wrapped up in the wonder and power of love. And this is only human love. The story of Romeo and Juliet, even when told by Shakespeare, pales in comparison to the divine love story. The story of divine foolishness: love between Creator and creation.

We well know that the course of true love does not run smoothly: the Fall. But does the Creator turn his back on creation after the Fall? Not at all. God's foolish love, God's passion, is to re-create: to do all God can for Creator and creation to be one again.

So the pounding heart of love, the heart of God is revealed to us in God Made Man, Jesus Christ. The throb of divine love pounds throughout Jesus' journey on earth—a journey of sacred and foolish love, commitment, rebellion against rigid conformity, passion, and crucifixion.

The cross: the ultimate case of misunderstanding between lovers—between Jesus and humankind's authority figures, too frightened to let go of how they think they ought to be loving God.

The cross: the greatest lovers' quarrel of all time. The passion of God to re-create creation, versus the passion of humankind to resist the power and will of Love Divine.

The cross: the death of God Made Man. In the words of an ancient Orthodox Good Friday hymn: "Today, he who wraps the heavens in the clouds is wrapped in the purple of mockery. He who hung the earth upon the waters is hung upon the Cross." Dare we dismiss as mere allegory or fanciful illustration Matthew's account of the Temple curtain being torn in two, the earthquake, tombs opening? For we are talking of the cross in all its sacred foolishness. We are talking nothing else but cosmic collision between Creator and creation.

The cross: a cosmic collision of utterly irresistible force; the foolish insistence of the divine lover to embrace, overcome, and consume all human resistance, to transform the reign of darkness into the victory of love.

The cross: the death of death itself. John Donne writes: "Death be not proud, for those whom thou thinkest thou dost overthrow, die not poor death, nor yet canst thou kill me. One short sleep past, we wake eternally, and death shall be no more."

But what does this mean for people such as the citizens of Kosovo? This foolishness of the cross, this victory of love? The death of death itself—in Kosovo?

The wonder of the cross, the wonder of divine foolishness, is that the means of God's death was utterly mundane. Crucifixion of the innocent by the Roman authorities was a commonplace event.

Hannah Arendt, writing about the Holocaust, observes that the ultimate horror of human evil is to be seen not in the spectacular—some sudden and utterly shocking outburst of evil. The ultimate horror of human evil, she says, is when evil becomes an ordinary, everyday, ongoing event. "The banality of evil," she calls it.

The wonder of God's foolish love is God's entry into the banality of human evil, the almost everyday event, crucifixion of the innocent. So there in the banality of ethnic cleansing (how commonplace the phrase has now become), there in the horror of Kosovo, is God, the lover of humankind, walking the streets and lanes of man-made hell, crying out like an insistent peddler: "Use my gifts, the free gifts of love, forgiveness, reconciliation. Through the power of my Spirit you can use my gifts . . . if you want to."

But who will hear the divine peddler foolishly hawking his wares in the name of love? In Kosovo we don't yet know. But elsewhere there are sure signs that the divine peddler's voice has indeed been heard. South Africa: the apartheid regime, now South Africa. Anyone who saw Bill Moyers' program about the horrors of apartheid and the work of the Truth and Reconciliation Commission, under the chairmanship of Archbishop Desmond Tutu, cannot fail to have been moved by the progress that is being made in the healing of that nation. Through the willingness of humankind, black and white, to respond to the divine peddler's call, the spring shoots of new life in Christ push their painful way, up through the dark and bloody soil of South Africa.

Here in Buffalo, an elderly woman prepares for her rapidly approaching death. She talks about her past life, the dark and fearsome mystery of the cancer-riddled present, and the certain peace and wonder of the life shortly to come. I sit there at her bedside marveling at her confidence, her inner strength; humbled by her absolute faith that it is not death she faces, but new life with her Lord and Savior.

South Africa, Buffalo: Both scenes bear witness to all that lies behind the cross. God's foolishness. God's passion. Dare I say, the eros of God: the cross thrust into creation. God determined to re-create at all costs. And the insistent call of the divine peddler, the call of the divine lover to the beloved, to you and me, is that we be partners with God in the foolish, sacred work of re-creation.

Stephen J. S. Smith is canon for congregational life
at St. Paul's Cathedral, Buffalo, New York.

EASTER DAY

Easter Terror

Matthew 28:1–10
J. Scott Barker

WHEN THE weather gets warm like this, I start running again. I am a fair-weather jogger: very disciplined about getting out three times a week, April through November, and totally wimpy about getting out during the cold months. I don't like running much. I never have. Some people say they get a "runner's high" from jogging, but the closest I've ever come to that is a vague feeling of accomplishment when I'm done: "Well, at least I got that over with." I run to stay in shape. So that my kids won't be able to beat me up when they get bigger. Running is a chore I do to stay healthy. I think of it as something that just has to be done: like paying taxes, shaving, or taking out the trash.

When I first arrived here at Resurrection, one of the things I was most thrilled about was having Miller Park right across the street. The beautiful old wooded golf course seemed like the perfect place to run at the end of my work day: way better than dodging the downtown traffic, where I'd been running until I came here. And so that's what I did. Around five o'clock on most nice days, I'd change into my running gear, lock the church behind me, and trot across the street to the park. Sometimes I'd run up and down Thirtieth Street, but the main part of my little run was always to make one big circuit around the park's edge. I probably hadn't been running at the park for two weeks when people began to caution me against it. One of the first people I met here in the neighborhood told me that, on a walk through the park early one morning, he had been beaten and robbed. He didn't think running around the park was such a hot idea. You probably remember that some time ago, there was also a murder in the park. That, too, made people worry about my jogging route.

But I told everybody not to worry. That shooting was about drugs, and it happened at night. So even though seeing crime tape up on the back side of the park made me nervous for a couple of days, I stuck to my guns, and kept on running. I am nothing if not determined: And I was determined to get out there three days a week, no matter what. It is a chore I am committed to, and I won't be deterred.

The two Marys were also in the mode of performing a "necessary chore" as they made their way to the tomb in the dark of that first Easter morning. A much more solemn and weighty chore than my exercising, for sure. Remember that Jesus was entombed in great haste on Good Friday. They had to get his body off the cross and into the grave quickly, before the sun went down and the Sabbath began. For the prohibition against working on the Sabbath—but especially against handling anything so unclean as a dead body—was very strong. The Gospels of Mark and Luke tell us that the women went to the tomb carrying spices. That is, they went to properly prepare Jesus' body for burial, a process that would include cleaning, anointing, and wrapping the corpse. A process they had not had time to even begin on Friday afternoon.

I imagine there was some fear associated with their duty. Remember that Jesus was killed as a kind of traitor, and an angry mob had demanded his execution. Remember that Peter was so scared of the mob he actually denied knowing Jesus rather than be exposed as one of his followers. I'll bet the women had some concern about going to Jesus' tomb that morning in the dark. But they were devoted followers of Jesus, and committed to the task. Though it was painful duty, and more than a little scary, perhaps, there was no doubt in their minds that it had to be done. And it had to be done right. And it had to be done now. And so off they went to the tomb. To perform a necessary chore.

On one very hot summer day, after I'd been running around the park for about a year, something scary happens to me. The run starts innocently enough. Since it is a blistering day, everybody is sitting on their porches in the homes around the edge of the park. I like hot days for this reason. I'll nod and say "Hi!" to folks as I lope past their homes. And though I don't really know anybody on my route, it's nice to say "Hey!"

to people, and imagine that they might be getting to recognize me. Well, on this scorching day, I am sweating like mad, very uncomfortable. As I head south along the backside of park, I notice across the street, about a half block ahead of me, a house with a porch full of loud young men. As I run closer, I can hear their excited voices saying things like "Do it, man!" "Get him!"

Now, I do not know if these guys are talking about me. Besides, there really is nowhere to go but straight ahead. So, although the scene doesn't feel quite right, I just keep on striding down the sidewalk, trying to look smooth, while sweat pours down my face, and makes my T-shirt stick and pull uncomfortably.

As I get closer to the house, to my dismay, a young man jumps over the edge of the porch and starts making his way across the yard of the house on a perfect diagonal, heading straight toward me. I sort of slyly look around me; but there's no other person or vehicle that he could be heading toward. When I look back there is no doubt: He is coming at me.

The two Marys know there is some risk involved in going to the tomb, but they make their way through the dark just the same. They are determined. Committed. They have this thing that simply has to be done. But at some point, their determination—their commitment to do the right thing and take care of Jesus' body—turns from firm resolve to knock-kneed terror. Imagine! They are making their way to the tomb when a great earthquake comes. And then an angel, whose appearance is "like lightning" comes before them. Is he scary? Oh, only a little bit: so scary that the big tough Roman guards hanging around the tomb are paralyzed with fear! And then the angel turns and speaks to the women (which we all know from watching Andrew on Touched by an Angel might not be a good sign!). The angel says, "Don't be afraid."

YAAAHH!

And then the angel is going to, like, comfort them, right? So he says, "I know that you are looking for Jesus, but he was raised from the dead. He's not here. Go see for yourselves." Now when an angel says, "Jump," you jump! And so the Marys look and, sure enough, Jesus' body is missing from the tomb. "See, I told you," says the angel. "Now, here's what you must do. Go and tell the disciples that he has been raised from the dead, and is going ahead to meet you in Galilee."

And the Bible says, "They left the tomb quickly with fear and great joy, and ran to tell his disciples." "Fear and great joy." We know what that means don't we? "I'm gettin' out of here!"

I've got to get out of here. That's what I am thinking at Miller Park that day. And for a second I believe I can do it. I may not be the speediest guy in the world, but I am a runner, and I run a lot. Also, I know how important motivation is when you're running. They say you can run twice as far on race day as you can in practice, just on sheer adrenaline. Well, I've got that adrenaline thing going, so I figure I am probably okay. Maybe the kid is totally harmless. Maybe he's seen me in my priest suit, and wants to hear about Jesus. So I figure I'll just give him the benefit of the doubt, but if he disrespects me or swings at me, we'll see just how fast I am. So I slow down to avoid a collision as he trots right up into my face.

"Greetings!" he says. And there is nothing wrong with his tone. And his eyes say, "I am not a scary guy."

But then he pulls a gun out from behind his back.

So now Mary One and Mary Two are on the run. And with "fear and great joy" they are getting away from that empty tomb as fast as they can. I imagine that, like me, they think for a second they can outrun the scary events in which they find themselves caught up. They probably think, "Wow! That was some weird exchange back there at that tomb, with those frightened guards, and that—whatever that guy was, all dressed in white. Thank God that's over with."

They think everything is going to be okay. Well, not exactly okay, because Jesus is still dead, and now his body is missing too; but at least "okay," insofar as they get away from that bizarre encounter at Jesus' grave. I imagine their hearts have just about slowed down to some kind of normal rhythm again when, as Matthew's story tells us, "Suddenly Jesus himself appeared and said, 'Greetings!'"

"Greetings!" the kid says. But I can't take my eyes off that gun. Suddenly, it doesn't seem so important that it's broad daylight, or that there are lots of people sitting around on their porches, or that I am a pretty fast runner. Suddenly my attitude about "It won't happen to me" seems pretty stupid. Because it is happening to me. I have a big, black gun pointed right at my chest. Suddenly I am face to face with the unthinkable.

Suddenly, the Marys are face-to-face with the unthinkable. Scary enough: the trial, the crucifixion, the earthquake, the darkness, the man at the tomb. But now this. This incomprehensible moment. A dead man raised? Jesus, alive? Christ with us? And what's that he's saying? "Greetings!" As if his very presence doesn't fill them with the worst imaginable terror! Not the kind where something extremely unlikely is happening, and so you have to deal with facing something you thought only happened to other people. But rather the kind of terror that results when something *impossible* is happening; and so you are made to deal with facing something you thought could *never* be. Something so unlikely, improbable, and just *out there* that the only way to make "sense" of it is to think: Surely this is a dream. But it is too real to be a dream. There is the sun beating down. And their feet sore from running.

And the smell of him. And the sight of his wounds. And his oddly calm greeting still ringing in their ears, "Greetings."

As I glance down Twenty-fourth Street for help, I wish it were a dream, but it is too real. There is the sun beating down. And my feet sore from running. And the smell of him. And the sight of the gun. And his oddly calm greeting still ringing in my ears: "Greetings!"

"What's he going to do," I wonder. "How is this going to happen?" And the kid says, "Are you hot?" And I am way too surprised to do anything but blurt out the truth, "Yeah!" "Do you want me to get you?" he asks, leveling the gun at my face.

Yep. It is a squirt gun. A big shiny black squirt gun that looks exactly like an Uzi. And I say with more relief and joy than he probably can begin to understand, "Oh yes! Hit me!"

It was a moment of transformation. Everything I thought was wrong: The kid I thought was a gangster was an angel of mercy. The gun I thought was a weapon of destruction was an instrument of peace. A confrontation I thought might cost me life turned out to be a graceful occasion of life abundant.

Christ was right there. And he whisked away my fear of death and substituted joy for living. As the trigger was pulled, I spun around in the beating sun, getting wetter and wetter, in a great wet baptism by fire that I will never ever forget. And as I did my little dance of joy—all the homeboys on the porch applauded. I never loved a stranger more, or felt better about a lukewarm bath. And I never ran with more joy than I did heading back to Church of the Resurrection from Miller Park that afternoon.

What Mary and Mary discovered that day—two thousand years before me—was that God cannot be contained. God is not bound by our rules . . . not hemmed in by our expectations . . . not constrained by human limitations. There is no fear that God cannot calm. There is no threat that God cannot shatter. There is no adversity or trial that God cannot overcome. That moment when they met Jesus on the road was a moment of transformation. A moment of discovery—everything they thought they knew was wrong.

The earthquake was not an omen of destruction, but a portent of God's power. The specter at the tomb was not a fraud or an angel of death, but a messenger of life. The cross of Good Friday that appeared to be a weapon of destruction was an instrument of peace. The confrontation that raised every hackle on their bodies, and had them fearing for their lives, turned out to be a joyful occasion to celebrate the victory of life over death—to share the joy of life abundant.

"Do not be afraid!" Jesus says this morning. Oh, and he means it! Many of you know this joy. You have experienced it when God has pulled you back from the edge of the abyss and surprised you—utterly surprised you—with a healing, or a reconciliation, or a relationship—or a resurrection—so fat with improbability and grace that it could only have one author. And if—bless your heart—this isn't a feeling that you have experienced, if this is a kind of joy that is foreign to you, then I invite you to accept Christ into your life, and get to know him a little better.

Because joy is what it's all about: throbbing, pulsing, panting, all-out joy! The kind of joy that makes you want to run, to run from your doubts and your worries and your hurts and into the arms of a loving and living God. The kind of joy that makes you want to just shout out to the world: we don't have to be afraid anymore! Jesus is alive! Christ is risen!

J. Scott Barker is rector of the Church of the Resurrection, Omaha, Nebraska.

THIRD SUNDAY OF EASTER

Bread

Luke 24:13–35
William W. Ryan

A FEW weeks ago we enjoyed a seder supper, prepared by our able and hard-working parish life volunteers. Perhaps you have attended another such dinner in the past. What I remember most about that dinner is being so hungry, and not being able to eat when I wanted to. We sat at table, and there was food in front of us, but we could not touch it. Leg of lamb was roasting in the ovens, with onions, garlic, and potatoes. The aroma wafting through the parish hall was making my knees weak. But we couldn't eat any of it. There was to be praying and singing first, followed by announcements. And still we couldn't eat

I think our Jewish leader, Avi Golub, was enjoying our predicament. He relished the part of the meal that included breaking the matzo, the unleavened bread. He would say, "Hold up the matzo, but don't eat it. Sing this song first." Then, grinning, he said, "Break off a piece, but you can't eat it yet. Say this prayer first." Then, almost laughing, "Give a piece to each person at your table. No, not yet, don't eat it! Now let me tell you a little bit about the history of the seder."

When it finally came time to have a nibble of matzo, it tasted like the finest bread ever baked. Manna from heaven could not have tasted better. Eventually, like all meals here at St. Mark's, we began a veritable feast. What a joy it was that evening, to break bread with one another.

There is nothing more wonderful than breaking bread with friends. In fact there is nothing purer, nothing more satisfying, than sharing a loaf. When one person who has a loaf breaks off a piece and gives it to someone else, it's not just eating. This act is fundamental to our faith. Everything else we do, or say, or think, or believe about God and Christ, about heaven and earth, follows after that foundational, structural act. Because you have something—a loaf. And what you have is significant to my growth and health and well-being. And you give some of what you have to me. And because of your act of giving, I grow, I am well, I live. Sharing a loaf is like eating a good breakfast in the morning. The rest of the day depends on it.

This loaf that we might share with others could be a warm greeting given to a stranger. This loaf could be a handshake, or a pat on the back, to someone who has had a bit of bad news in her life. It could be the money that we were going to spend on a new outfit for ourselves, but now goes to the local food bank. This loaf could be as simple as reading a story to your child or grandchild. Or it could be as powerful as telling the story of the life, death, and resurrection of Jesus Christ to those who are hearing it for the first time.

Whatever the loaf, when it is broken and given to one as a gift from another, something wonderful happens. Light bulbs pop up over our heads. Our eyes open wide with understanding and assurance. Like Dr. Seuss's Grinch, whose heart grew three sizes larger when he found out he couldn't steal Christmas, our hearts grow a bit bigger. And, like the travelers on the road to Emmaus, we, too, are enlightened. We hear something fantastic. We learn something wondrous. It makes our hearts burn and our souls ache. It sends us out into the world, nourished, fortified, ready to break more loaves with more people.

The breaking of bread is the chain letter that works, the pyramid scheme that doesn't collapse. The breaking of bread is how, three hundred years after the events on the road to Emmaus, the entire known world had encountered the Christian gospel. For the gospel was a loaf too wonderful for the first Christians to keep to themselves. They just had to share it. And from their broken bread, you and I understand and now believe that some women went to the tomb early one morning, and did not find the body of Christ. But instead saw a vision of angels who said that Christ was alive. From their broken bread, you and I take their good news, and share it with others, along with our hearts, our riches, our lives.

Because of the broken bread, which to some might look like the discarded crumbs of a feast long ago ended, we, like Peter, devote ourselves to the teaching, the fellowship, and the prayers, of God's holy church. Because of the simple act of breaking bread, and sharing loaves.

Recently I read the John Grisham book, *Street Lawyer*. The story is about a rich and successful Washington, D.C. attorney who, because of some life changing experiences, finds himself defending the rights of the homeless in the D.C. area. The scenes take place in and out of homeless shelters and soup kitchens in Washington. I was struck by the description of a young woman and her three children eating a meal together. The four of them had nowhere to stay. They slept in an old car, and made their way around best they could. One of the difficult issues of homelessness is that families are often separated. Kids are sent to foster homes, and mothers sometimes are not permitted access to their own children. It's so difficult to keep a family together without a roof over their heads. This particular family was struggling mightily to stay together. In one scene they are huddled together in the corner of the dining area of a soup kitchen.

It is the first time all day that they had been together. And before them they have bowls of soup, and stale, hard rolls. The older kids are picking at their plates. The mother is trying to get the baby to eat something. She herself takes bites in between correcting her children. "Sit up. Say thank you." But in this particular moment of time, when bread is broken in fellowship with one another, these four very poor people proclaim to the world that they, too, are a family. They, too, are loved by God. They, too, are blessed through the breaking of the bread. What will happen to them tomorrow may be tragic. But at least for a moment, in the breaking of bread, they sense communion and fellowship. And somehow, through the breaking of bread, a shared meal together, they have the strength to make it through one more night, and they hope that things will get better.

In the breaking of the bread we, too, find our hope. At the altar rail, gathered together with opened hands and wishful hearts, at the dinner table, united as a family after a long day of separation, in the parish hall, as the Body of Christ comes together for laughter and fellowship, we too find our strength and our hope in the simple act of breaking bread together. For when bread is broken, Christ is known, and comes among us, to mend broken hearts, broken souls, broken lives. The Lord has risen indeed, and has come among us.

William W. Ryan is associate rector of St. Mark's Church,
Venice, Florida.

Fruitful Connections

1 Peter 3:8–18; John 15:1-8
Susan W. Klein

WE ARE born needing to connect. Babies come out of the womb some-how knowing how to grip your finger, your hair, your sweater, with the strength of a tiger, letting you know that the real squeeze is about to begin, the one that captures your heart for all of your natural life. When things go well, the mother and father strike up an immediate connection with their child; and within weeks, the baby is smiling when they smile, laughing when they laugh.

Nothing can take the place of this early connecting business. When you see children who have been abandoned or seriously damaged early on, it is as though you are trying to phone someone and keep getting the wrong number. Often they are unable to connect for the rest of their lives.

We are all used to the phrase made popular by Barbara Streisand: "people who need people." And when it goes well for us, we thrive. Fruitful connections give us warmth, nurture, courage, hope, even in dark and uncertain times. How many times have I heard people say that, though they had few material goods growing up, they never felt poor because of the happiness and love in their families. Fruitful connections are found wher-ever the love of God dwells. Fruitful connections reveal the love of God. And on this day, we celebrate the ways our mothers and grandmothers, and all the mother figures in our lives, have nurtured the love of God within us.

Not all connections, though, are good for us. Sometimes our need to connect can be so strong that we plug into the first empty socket we find. And we find it to be a very dangerous or bad connection. The girl gets on the motorcycle of the exciting older man, and is never heard from again. The boy is befriended by someone as lonely as he is, and finds a companion full of hatred, full of rage. The retired teacher is bilked out of her savings by the charming salesperson at her door.

We are all affected throughout life by our connections with other people. We are vulnerable to others from birth to death. Once I visited a woman with Alzheimer's who was living in a nursing home. The attendants always seemed brusque, cold, even angry. As we walked down the hall, we passed a man in a wheelchair being pushed by an attendant. "Oh look,", the woman said with the perception that impaired people sometimes have, "they are taking out the garbage." She knew, in her own way, how to describe the contempt she felt in the ones connected to her.

Good or bad, we seek connections, and we are affected by them more than we realize throughout our lives. That is why I love the image Jesus uses to talk about the church. "I am the vine," he says, "and you are the branches."

With that living, vibrant image, Jesus uses the language of connection to paint a picture of the relationships found in the church of God. A vine is what provides food and water to the branches. It is what connects them to their roots. A vine is the umbilical cord to the branches. When the branch becomes disconnected from the vine, it becomes history.

But a vine does not just work vertically. A vine is what connects the branches to each other. What Jesus is describing is a dynamic system of nurture, feedback, growth, groundedness. He is the vine, giving himself to the branches, the disciples, helping them grow, flourish, provide fruit. They are dependent on him. As the vine, he is also the means of their interdependence, of their connection with each other.

Often the church is not fruitful. Over the years I have heard too many stories of churches that violated the boundaries of their members, that ostracized those who criticized, that shamed those who disagreed with their theology, programs, and policies. Hearing these stories reminds me that bugs attack, that weeds choke life, that gardeners fail to nurture and water plants.

But when a church is faithful to this image of Jesus, its disciples are productive beyond measure—as individuals, and as a community. The outcasts are welcomed, the hungry fed. The young are prevented from getting too lost; the older ones are able to be found. When a church is faithful to this image of dependence and interdependence, love is a palpable presence in the community and beyond it. There is goodwill and good humor. There is generosity and inclusiveness. When the branches and vines are all working together, their common worship recycles the carbon dioxide and toxins of our culture into the pure oxygen of holiness.

When branches and vines are faithful, the words of Peter come true: ". . . [A]ll of you, have unity of spirit, sympathy, love for one another, a tender heart, and a humble mind. Do not repay evil for evil or abuse for abuse; but, on the contrary, repay with a blessing. It is for this you were called—that you might inherit a blessing."

Last week I met a vicar of a mission whose church building was burned down by a quite disturbed young man living in the neighborhood. After his arrest and conviction, the members of this mission decided that they had a duty, as members of the vine, to visit him in prison. One by one they go each week, taking him gifts, praying with him, listening. They are doing the work of the fruitful branches. Repaying their abuser with blessings, they are receiving blessing upon blessing.

A parish community can be full of connections, not only in the present, but in the past. As I walk around our property, I am reminded of many disciples and their work and ministry. I am reminded of Paul and Mary, in whose memory a garden was planted. I think of their goodness, their long-lived marriage, their faithfulness. I think of Jim, and his ministry of teaching, as I look at the altar his wife helped to design. I think of the Irish saint named Aidan to whom our parish is dedicated. I think of the ways he spread the gospel among the pagans of his day, serving humbly and patiently, teaching, preaching, and pastoring in the light and love of Christ.

Kneeling here, my prayers often take me in gratitude to God for the many saints I knew growing up, the ones I've met in the churches I've served, the ones I've met on my travels. I think of the disciple I met in Ghana who farmed all day in her village, carrying water in a jug on her head from the well in the next village, a disciple who was starting a tiny mission church by leading Bible study in the evenings. Being a part of the vine reminds us of the whole communion of saints, the vine and its branches universal. It says we are not alone. Throughout history, fruitful branches have been as numerous as the stars in the sky.

Finally, the vine and its branches speak of the love of God, a God who is present in and through all of our connections. Being a member of the vine doesn't give us an exclusive sense of the love of God, but I wonder how, without it, anyone comes to know this One in our midst.

As we are connected to this vine, the Risen and Living Christ still runs through our blood like sap, nurturing us, sustaining us with community, giving our new and old branches more fruit than we could ever believe possible. And in a world that is hungry and thirsty, what could be better than to be a branch on this vine?

Susan W. Klein is rector of St. Aidan's Church in Malibu, California.

THE DAY OF PENTECOST

A Life Not Our Own

John 14:8–17
Raynor Anderson

I CAN'T get the film *Saving Private Ryan* out of my mind. It's a gut-wrenching movie, showing the gruesome, bloody horrors of war (there were scenes I couldn't watch). But the movie haunts me; and it has taken time to figure out why. It's about Christ—although Jesus Christ only appears in the film as a swear word. It's a totally secular movie about a totally frustrating and horrible human situation that is deeply spiritual.

A mother has lost four sons in the war. Word comes to a general that her only remaining son (the youngest) is fighting in France. The general, for public relations reasons, gives orders that the boy be found and brought home alive. The job is given to a platoon of Rangers, battle-hardened experts in warfare. They go across German lines in search of this young kid, Private Ryan. Eventually they find him. He doesn't want to leave his squad, but he must. The Rangers all wonder why they are risking their lives for this kid, who means nothing to the war effort. Saving him will not end the war any sooner.

They start back toward American lines and have various skirmishes with German units. In these, despite their skill and selfless heroism, they are all eventually killed. As he dies, the captain of the platoon (Tom Hanks), says to the kid, "All these have died saving you. Do good with your life."

The next scene is fifty years later. The kid, Ryan, is now an old man who has returned to the cemetery in Europe where these Rangers who died saving him are buried. He's standing before the captain's grave staring at his name on the white cross that is the headstone. He is white-haired and stoop-shouldered. His life is almost done. His wife, children, and grandchildren are in the background talking casually, unaware that they are standing on what is, to Ryan, holy ground. The old man suddenly pulls himself, ramrod erect, to attention; and salutes the captain's grave, with all the military respect and honor of the young soldier that once he was. His wife comes up behind him. He turns to her. With a deep need to know, he asks: "Am I a good man?"

"Don't be silly, dear," she says, nonchalantly, "of course you are."

"No, I'm serious, have I been a good man? Have I done good?" The camera pulls back and up, showing thousands of white crosses. End of movie.

A man plunges into a river to save a drowning child, but in doing so loses his own life. Someone tries to overpower a crazed gunman in a shooting spree in a McDonalds, and dies in the process, but saves others. A fireman pulls a child from a burning building, but is, himself, consumed by the flames. Such things are rare, but they happen. What a difference it must make to me, if my life has been saved by another!

We all love our independence, self-reliance. I don't want to owe anything to anyone, I want to do my own thing, to "Do it my way." But when my life has been saved by another's, I continually have to confront the fact that my "way" is shaped by theirs. I do what I do because of them. I recognize an internal imperative to live as meaningful, honorable, and good a life as their death for me was meaningful, honorable, and good. The life of the one who gave me mine back is shown in how I live. That's why the elderly Ryan, asks "Am I a good man? Did I 'do good'?"

Jesus died a long, long time ago so that we might live eternally. He was sent behind enemy lines to rescue us, to bring us back alive (and not just for publicity purposes). He even had a platoon of Rangers (apostles) with him, not one of which died a natural death. He commanded us to "do good," and empowered us to do so. His words in John's Gospel are these: "If you love me, you will keep my commandments. And I will ask the Father, and he will give you another Advocate, to be with you forever. This is the Spirit of truth, whom the world cannot receive, because it neither sees him nor knows him. You know him, because he abides in him, and he will be in you."

In a world where most people believe that, even if God does exist, he long ago drifted away, does he live in us and we in him?

If you, like me, believe Jesus has inspired countless people to acts of self-sacrifice; if you believe the humbling, self-giving love Jesus taught is what you need; if you believe that truth, meaning, and a worthwhile life (the "do good") is found in living not for yourself alone; then you do your best to live as meaningful, honorable, and good a life as Jesus' death was, and his resurrection is.

The Lord does not require us to stand at his grave and snap off a military salute. He does ask us to love one another as he has loved us: caring for the sick, protecting the weak, honoring others, and thereby honoring him.

Our lives are not our own. They belong to the one who saved them.

Raynor Anderson is missioner at St. Paul's Mission of the Deaf, West Hartford, Connecticut.

TRINITY SUNDAY

God, The *Moved* Mover

Genesis 1:1–2:3
Roger Alling

SEVERAL YEARS ago when I went to church on Trinity Sunday, the preacher said that the Trinity was a great and wonderful mystery but, unfortunately, it was too difficult to understand. We should just stand before the mystery of it in awe and worship.

Well, I agree that, after all of our words, we will be forced to stand in awe, and worship before God the Trinity. But I am more optimistic than that other preacher. I do think that we can understand some things about God as Trinity; and that, as Christians, we will be the better for it if we do.

When my children were growing up we used to ask questions, like: "What are things made of?" and "Who made the things we see?" It got the boys thinking about the world around them, and about where everything came from. It got us talking about things like atoms; and it got us talking about God. We couldn't see atoms. Nor could we see God. But the questions helped us to think about both.

It was a fixed and static world that those discussions painted for my children. Atoms were the fixed and reliable building blocks from which all other material was constructed; and God was the stable and fixed starting point for everything that was or ever could be.

These were not new ideas. Centuries ago in Greece, philosophers first talked about the atoms being the smallest things in the world, the building blocks for everything else. These ancient Greeks also had ideas about God. Aristotle called God the Unmoved Mover. He believed that God acted to put everything else into motion, but that God's own self was not moved. God caused all the action; but God was never acted upon.

I suspect that many of us are still under the influence of these Greek thinkers. We may not be aware of the fact that their ideas, while insightful, no longer reflect all of what we now know about atoms. Nor do they reflect our best understanding about God.

Let's deal with the atoms first. We still use the word *atom*, but we know much more about them now than those ancient thinkers ever could have imagined. We know now that the atom itself is a marvelous universe in miniature. With the nucleus at its center, the tiny subatomic particles whirl around the nucleus like the planets circle our sun. Atoms are neither fixed nor static. Indeed, within themselves they contain immense amounts of energy and power.

Jews and Christians developed very different ideas about God than those held by the Greeks. Like the Greeks, they understood God as the One who created the universe and set all things in motion. They did not believe, however, that God just made the world and then left it at that. They believed that God kept in touch with creation. God cared for the world, and interacted with everything made. Certainly what God did had an impact upon the world, but the reverse was true as well. The world also had an impact upon God. God felt anger at injustice and sin. God grieved over our failings and our lack of trust. God showed compassion and love for the world and its creatures.

God was the Mover, but not the Unmoved Mover. God was the Mover who was moved.

At a critical time God sent God's only begotten Son into the world for its redemption. Then, in a subsequent act, God sent the Holy Spirit who was and is an everlasting source of strength and blessing for the world. The Mover was moved to create. The Mover was moved to save. The Mover was moved to bless.

Because of this we came to know God in a new way. We came to know God as, God the Father, Creator; God the Son, Redeemer; and God the Holy Spirit, Sanctifier. We came to know God as the Holy and Blessed Trinity.

Our first ideas about God as Trinity came about because of the rich experiences that God's people had of God over many hundreds of years. God revealed Godself as Trinity by virtue of God's dealings with us and with our world.

It was only later that some Christians developed the Trinity idea even further. They asked themselves what God might be like in and of Godself. They believed that God existed before the worlds were made, so they asked, "What was God like then?" In what sense could God be Trinity when there was no world yet with which to interact? God's relationship with the world helps us to see what God *does*, but how can we come to understand who God is, independently from our own experience—of ourselves, of each other, and of the world?

Remember the atom, that tiny unit we used to think of as a static building block. We now understand the atom as a dynamic, tiny world in itself, full of energy and power. So it is with God on a far grander scale.

St. Augustine, a fourth-century bishop in North Africa, probably developed this understanding of the Trinity as well as anyone. Augustine believed that, at heart, God is Community. This community of Father, Son, and Holy Spirit is an eternal dynamic relationship.

In that relationship, the Father loves the Son. The Son responds in love to the Father. The bond of love that comes from the Father, and returned by the Son, is the Holy Spirit of God, which is always moving from the one to the other, and back again. This love is what keeps the Father and the Son together and energized. This giving and receiving of love, and the unity which that love creates, is the very heart, power, and soul of God.

These dynamic interchanges between Father and Son are what we mean when we say that God is love. They are what we mean when we talk about eternal life. Eternal life is God's life. Eternal life is the inner and everlasting life of God. The Trinity is the eternal community of God. Father loving Son. Son loving Father. Love binding the two together. When we get close to God, we join in that life. When we die, we are part of that life forever.

The fact that there is a world at all arises from the loving and energetic nature of God. God is Community; and it is God's business to bring other communities into being. The story of how God does this is to be found in the Scriptures and heritage of Israel, and of the church. One of the parts of this magnificent memory and story was read as our first lesson this morning from the book of Genesis. God loved the world into being, and was satisfied with its goodness when God rested on that first Sabbath Day.

When God's good creation suffered the twin corruptions of sin and death, God was moved by this threat and danger, and sent Jesus Christ. Through Christ's life and ministry, death and resurrection, God initiated the "re-creation" of Creation.

As the ministry of Jesus drew to a close, Jesus gathered his disciples on a mountaintop to turn his work over to them. Having promised the Holy Spirit soon to come, he charged them to go into all the world and to make disciples of all nations, baptizing in the name of the Trinity: Father, Son, and Holy Spirit.

The God who is Community calls people into community, and sends them out to build communities everywhere. We are one of those communities. Often we think of ourselves in the church and in parishes as pretty small change. We wonder sometimes how important we are in the grand scheme of things. However, we may have more power than we think.

As we grow, we change our ideas about atoms, and we change our ideas about God. Perhaps we also need to change our ideas about ourselves as well.

The tiny atom is not a static brick but a tiny storehouse of power waiting to be released. God is not static either, but full of dynamism and power. Perhaps the same might be said of a parish church. It, too, may be a storehouse of power just waiting to be released. A church is a microcosm of nothing less than the eternal life of God the Trinity. At its very center is the dynamic love of God; and you and I circle round it like subatomic particles, energized by God and held together by God's love and grace.

Who knows what power may be released from us for God's continuing work in the world? Who knows what Communities of God we may be able to bring into being for the God who is Community?

Roger Alling is co-editor of this volume.

PROPER EIGHT

Family Values

Matthew 10:34–42
J. Barry Vaughn

SEVERAL YEARS ago former Vice President Dan Quayle gave a famous speech in which he criticized the main character of the TV show *Murphy Brown* for having a child out of wedlock. Instead of setting such a bad example, he said, television should exemplify "family values." Al Gore made family values a central theme in the speech launching his bid to become president of the United States.

"Family values" has become the rallying cry of the religious right. In many ways, I think they are onto something important. Drug abuse, crime, education, divorce, unwanted children, domestic abuse—certainly better parenting and healthier families would do a lot to alleviate these and other social problems.

So, of course, we expect Jesus to be on the side of family values. What did Jesus have to say about family values? "Do not think that I have come to bring peace on earth; I have not come to bring peace, but a sword. For I have come to set a man against his father, and a daughter against her mother, and a daughter-in-law against her mother-in-law; and a man's foes will be those of his own household."

Uh oh . . . I hope the Christian Coalition doesn't hear about this. They might try to have Jesus banned from the Internet, or at least have the National Endowment for the Humanities cut off his funding.

I'm not trying to be facetious, but it's a little difficult to see Jesus waving the banner of family values, as understood by many on the religious right. Jesus' relationship with his own family seems to have been very troubled, and the trouble started at the very beginning. When Joseph learned that his fiancée Mary was pregnant before the marriage, he seriously considered calling the whole thing off. He was only dissuaded by a direct message from God delivered in a dream.

When he was twelve years old, Jesus remained in the Temple, rather than returning to Nazareth with Mary and Joseph. When they found the boy missing from their traveling party, they returned to the Temple and found him conversing with the learned men. Mary scolded Jesus rather sharply: "Son, why have you treated us so? Behold, your father and I have been looking for you anxiously"(Luke 2:48b, RSV). And Jesus replied, equally sharply, "Did you not know that I must be in my Father's house?" (Luke 2:49b, RSV). By identifying the Temple as "his Father's house," rather than Joseph's house in Nazareth, the twelve-year-old Jesus was already declaring his independence from his family. Wouldn't that have been an interesting Gospel reading last week for Father's Day?

When Jesus finally launched his ministry of teaching and miraculous cures, his family believed that he was possessed by a demon and tried to seize him, and bring him home with them. It was as though a family in our day were trying to abduct and deprogram a child who had joined a cult. When Jesus learned what his family was trying to do, he looked around at his disciples and said, "Who are my mother and my brothers? . . . whoever does the will of God is my brother, and sister, and mother." In effect, he disowned his earthly family, and announced the creation of a new, spiritual family.

Jesus and family values are an uneasy combination. Jesus himself was not married. Between the beginning of his ministry and his crucifixion, his family consisted of a motley group of disciples that included both men and women. Many of them seem to have abandoned their own families. The Gospels tell us that when Jesus called Peter and James and John, they dropped their fishing nets and followed him. In other words, they simply walked away from jobs and families to follow an itinerant prophet. This "family" that followed Jesus wandered from place to place. They seem to have supported themselves by asking for handouts. No wonder Jesus made the authorities nervous!

Now, don't misunderstand. Jesus never endorsed disobedience to parents, or encouraged husbands and wives to leave each other. And Jesus was no advocate of irresponsibility. But the teachings of Jesus radically challenged the idea of family in the first century, and perhaps in our world, too.

In the first century, family was everything. One was a Jew because one's mother was Jewish. One didn't choose the Jewish faith; one was born into it. That was why Nicodemus found Jesus so puzzling. "You must be born again," Jesus said to Nicodemus; and the learned Nicodemus replied, "How can this be? Can one enter again into one's mother's womb?"

Nicodemus saw no need for a second birth. He had been born a Jew and a Pharisee. No greater heritage was imaginable. We've become so accustomed to the phrase "born again" that we do not see what a revolutionary idea it was. It implied a radical rejection of the social-religious structure. One was to be born again not by blood but by the Spirit. One was to be born not into an earthly family, but into a spiritual one. One's earthly ancestors became irrelevant.

It was not just first-century Judaism that made the family central. It was true of the Roman Empire, as well. Family was everything. The family was the central institution in Rome. The father of a family was known as the *pater familias*, and he had almost absolute power over those in his household. But Jesus taught his disciples to call no one father except God. With a stroke, Jesus severed the ties that bound his disciples both to their earthly families, and to the larger societies of which families were, and are, the basic units.

"I have not come to bring peace, but a sword. I will set son against father and daughter against mother. . . ." Jesus came to found an entirely new kind of family. And it didn't take long before first the Jewish authorities and later the Roman authorities realized just how dangerous his ideas were.

A tribe is just an extension of the family or a collection of families. It is odd at the end of the twentieth century to find tribalism reasserting itself. The conflicts in Northern Ireland and the Middle East and above all the war in Kosovo are tribal wars. In a sense, they are family warfare. Protestant families against Catholic families. Muslim families against Jewish families. Orthodox Christian families against Muslim families. People are hated and killed simply because of who their parents and grandparents were.

At their best, families are places of love and warmth and nurture. And I venture to say that the healthiest families are those in which there is enough love, not only for those who have a claim to it by their birth, but also for those outside the circle of the family.

Jesus challenges us, challenges our families, to make room for the outsider. "Whoever welcomes you welcomes me, and whoever welcomes me welcomes the one who sent me. Whoever receives a prophet because he is a prophet shall receive a prophet's reward, and whoever receives a righteous man because he is a righteous man shall receive a righteous man's reward."

We are surrounded by angels in disguise. God is constantly probing at us and our families to see if our love excludes or includes, if we will constrict the circle of our love or open our arms wide.

How do we make room for the prophet, the righteous person, the one who comes to us representing God? We can include the homeless and the poor simply by recognizing them, smiling, saying a word, acknowledging that they are human beings. We include them when we make up a budget for our family that includes contributing to services that feed the hungry and house the homeless.

Jesus challenges our idea of family values because he preached a gospel of love without limits. Receive the prophet and the righteous person into your home as though you were receiving the very messenger of God, because that's exactly what you are doing.

Nowhere does Jesus encourage neglect of family. Rather, he asks us to love the poor, the hungry, and the homeless alongside our own parents and children. Jesus preached a "both/and" love, not an "either/or" love.

Did Jesus preach an impossible ethic? Yes. Does that mean that the bar is set so high that we might as well not even try? Not at all. Instead, Jesus expects us to learn to love by loving those in our families, and then extending that love to those outside, to those with no claim on our love, to those whom no one loves.

God put us in families because families are schools of love. Our families are schools of love, because it's very difficult to love someone you share a bathroom with! We are put in families because it's usually easiest to love those who are similar to us but, unfortunately, that's where we stop all too often. Loving those whom we know, loving people who love us, is only love's most basic arithmetic, but Jesus challenges us to go on and learn love's advanced calculus. We must love our families, to be sure, but that is only the first step on love's journey, a journey whose ultimate destination is to learn to love those who are completely different from us and perhaps even repellent to us.

Love your spouse. Love your children. Love your parents. Love your sisters and brothers. Love yourself. But don't let your love stop at the front door. Instead, keep your hearts and your homes wide open, because Jesus is coming to knock on your door.

J. Barry Vaughn is rector of St. Peter's Church of Germantown, Phildelphia, Pennsylvania.

PROPER TEN

Sowing with Spiritual Ecology

Matthew 13:1–9, 18–23
Sue Singer

"LISTEN! A sower went out to sow."

A sower in a successful, late-twentieth-century agribusiness went out. And he had well-tilled fields, on land that had been prepared for planting. He had fields with regular boundaries, of an optimum size for the crop. He took a seed drill to put in one seed every so often, in ruler-straight rows. He had irrigation and fertilizer, and an automated tiller to deal with the weeds between rows. He thinned the crop so the best specimens could grow to full maturity. And he kept a careful record of the yield, so he would know what to do differently next year, for better results. What a smart, sensible, cost-effective, efficient sower!

But when God sows, the picture is very different: This is old-fashioned, broadcast sowing, seed flung in the air by the handful. It lands where it will. There is seed everywhere. There are no field boundaries, no carefully prepared ground. The whole world is the field; the seed is sown indiscriminately on all kinds of ground—rocks, thin soil, the main road, the weed patch. And some makes it to the good ground, too.

The rain and the snow fall indiscriminately on the earth. Everything is allowed to grow. Nothing is thinned out and discarded. And finally, the harvest is a delight, whatever it is: a hundredfold return, sixty, thirty. It doesn't matter; it's the harvest!

What a God we have! What an impractical, indiscriminate, wildly generous God, flinging the seed of the Kingdom far and wide, including the whole world in the farm, ignoring the boundaries, letting the seed have a try anywhere. Who knows, one day even the desert might bloom! Letting it grow without constraint, sending the rain and snow in utter confidence that it will go where it is needed, rejoicing in the harvest— good and bad, expected and unexpected.

"Listen! A sower went out to sow."

The parables of Jesus were designed to do exactly what this parable does: to turn upside down our preconceived notions of what the Kingdom of a decent, self-respecting God will look like. If we had the ordering of God's Kingdom, it would probably look a lot like the fields of the agribusiness employee: orderly, controlled, full of the deserving and the good and the worthwhile people, a place where there are clear boundaries between right and wrong, clear answers to straightforward questions, rules applied without exceptions, and an eye to maximizing the overall yield of righteousness.

It's good we're not in charge! Partly because none of us would actually get in if God's Kingdom only admitted people who deserved to be there. But also because fields that are ruthlessly cleared, heavily cropped, and overly cultivated tend to end up dead—dust bowls in which nothing can grow.

God's approach makes better sense ecologically. Wild generosity with the seed, abundant rain and sun, and tolerance for a great diversity of habitat and plant life tend to produce a flourishing, resilient landscape where abundance and beauty flourish in all sorts of unlikely places.

And God's approach makes much better sense spiritually, too. You see, we are not dealing with a decent, self-respecting God here at all. Thank goodness! We are not dealing with a God who is at all concerned about rules, boundaries, and right answers. We are dealing with a God whose nature is abundance and self-emptying love, a God who is most God-like in the act of giving God's own self away.

Our God has a complete lack of self-respect. Our God scatters seeds with indiscriminate abundance, without looking to see if they are likely to bear fruit. Our God sends the rain and the snow on everyone, without regard to merit. Our God is so concerned that we don't waste our money on the things that will not satisfy us, that he invites us to eat and drink all we want for free.

Throughout his earthly career Jesus was always running into the religious authorities of his day, those who wanted to put fences round God's Kingdom, to limit who could come in, to judge people on the basis of their merits and whether they were likely to produce a good crop of righteous deeds.

But Jesus loved hanging out with those whose only virtue was that they knew their need of God. His favorite parties were those to which everyone was invited. He told scandalous parables that reversed everyone's expectations about what God was up to in the world, and he ended up hanging on a cross and rising from a tomb so that new life could burst in on the whole world for free.

God didn't raise Jesus from the dead for a select and deserving few. God doesn't redeem us and offer us eternal life because we deserve it. God doesn't pick us up and pour out forgiving grace upon us time after time because we deserve it. God does those things because God can't help loving us, because that is the kind of God we have—a Sower who has a vision of the whole world as a blooming, fertile, fruitful field, and who is prepared to sow the costly seed of redeeming love in the world by great handfuls in order to make that vision a reality.

If we know this Good News about God to be true, if we have experienced it in our own lives, if we live it out every week at this table where everyone is welcome, then we, too, will want to be sowers, indiscriminately loving, generous, hopeful sowers and sharers of the grace we have received ourselves.

I read two articles recently that made me think very hard about how difficult it is to do this, and how important it is to try. The first article, in a national newspaper, described how the president was planning to visit some of the poorest regions of this country to meet with community leaders. The purpose of the visits was to discover how the people living there in poverty could be enabled to become consumers in our economy. They were seen as a great untapped market for goods and services. Opportunities for the poorest to enjoy the blessings of work and dignity and a portion of the good things most of us take for granted were seen solely in terms of the return they would give, the boost they would provide to "the market." Anything more contrary to the way God operates I could not imagine—anything more opposed to the love that gives without thought of return, to the grace that wants the best for every beloved person without thought of how they can repay, to the Sower who broadcasts the good seed in all places.

The second article was in a much smaller publication—the newsletter of the San Bruno Catholic Worker. It described a phone call received from a woman who wanted to bring a group to help out at their dining room. Peter Steihler, the writer of the article and the director of the dining room, says, "I told her the days we were open, how many people we serve, and how her group could serve. Then hesitantly she asked, 'You don't have the same people all the time, do you? I mean, the people there aren't the type who aren't trying to improve themselves, are they?'"

Peter's article went on to address, in eloquent and honest and helpful terms, the structural issues in our economy and society that lie behind the existence of a large group of people who do in fact need help most of the time just to survive. He wrote about our corporate lack of will in relation to affordable housing, secure and permanent employment, and ways to care for the weakest members of society—precisely those whom we can so easily see as "rocky ground," weedy soil, unlikely to produce a good harvest and therefore not worthy of being sown.

Judging people on the basis of the "harvest" they produce is a spiritual viewpoint that we are called to avoid at all costs, because it is so antithetical to the way God has operated in our own lives and in the world.

We're invited instead to be generous, to give and to serve freely, to treat everyone as deserving because they are, simply by virtue of being a person, created in God's image and infinitely loved by God, just as we are. We're called to sow grace and freedom and love and help freely and with abandon, without calculation of the return, with something of the joy of God's own generosity, because that is the way our world is being redeemed, despite all our talk of "market forces" and despite every appearance to the contrary.

I was so proud yesterday to see this way of thinking and living in action here at All Saints'. The Saturday brunch program (open to anyone who wants to come) was serving beans as a side dish with the pasta and salads. The beans had come out of cans, and the cans had come from the food bank, but everyone was eating the beans with such obvious enjoyment that some of the helpers commented on this to the cook.

"Well," he said, "when I saw it would only be beans, I went and got four big yellow onions and a couple boxes of brown sugar, and I sautéed the onions and added the brown sugar and some tomato sauce, and got it good and hot, and then I put in the beans. I wanted to make it as good as possible."

Four yellow onions and a couple boxes of brown sugar—small seeds of God's Kingdom, signs of God's generosity, icons of the lavishness of grace and love that we are called to share, at all times, in all places, with all people, just because we have a God who will stop at nothing to "make it as good as possible" for us and for the whole world.

Sue Singer is education coordinator in the
Episcopal Diocese of California.

PROPER THIRTEEN

Exchanging Abundance

Romans 8:35–39, Matthew 14:13–21
Amy McCreath

I HAVE brought with me today my favorite symbol of abundance. In Kikuyu it is called a *kiodo*. I lived for a year in a Kenyan village. A woman who sold beans in the market every Thursday made it for me. This one is of sisal and wool—wool that I chose. It is considered very fancy by Kikuyu standards. Most kiodos are made of sisal and plastic—recycled plastic bags. Each kiodo is different—as each woman who carries one is different. As they walk along the road, women in the village can be identified by their kiodos from a distance.

Women carry their kiodos everywhere and use them for many things. My favorite memories of kiodos center on visiting friends. Whenever a Kikuyu woman goes to visit a neighbor, relative, or friend, she fills her kiodo with whatever happens to be growing on the farm, or whatever happens to be on the shelves in her kitchen. She overfills it, then covers it with a little knitted covering, so that no one can see what's inside. When she arrives at the home of her host, in a casual way, without comment or ceremony, she hands the kiodo to the woman of the house. The kiodo is taken to the kitchen and emptied of its contents. The host says nothing about it. At the end of the visit, the kiodo reappears from the kitchen, this time full of whatever is in the host's garden, or on the shelves in her kitchen. Again, no ceremony. No "Thank you." No exclamations.

This custom goes back centuries. It does not depend on anything. Kiodos are exchanged between rich and poor, in times of plenty and in times of drought or need, between very good friends, between perfect strangers. Kiodos are a given. They are always exchanged, always full. Every silent exchange speaks volumes about the faith of the people. They say, "I always have something to give, and I am always open to receiving." In an area of the world often characterized as needy or underdeveloped, where life is precarious and no one has a bank account or an IRA, such sharing can be life-saving. Through the exchange, the people help God set a table in the wilderness.

About ten years ago, kiodos came to the United States in the form of the "Kenya bag". These more sophisticated versions of the kiodo became quite popular as purses; perhaps some of you still have yours. There is nothing wrong with the way we use these bags, but they do lose something in translation. In the United States, Kenya bags hold things like car keys, checkbooks, day-runners, maybe a Diet Coke. Useful, legitimate things; but they all serve the bag's owner. If I arrived at a dinner party in Glendale and dumped the contents of my purse onto the host's kitchen table, I would get some strange glances. My host would never think to put her car keys, wallet, and Filofax into my purse, then hand it back to me!

But what if we *did* use our Kenya bags like the Kikuyu use kiodos? What might we bring to our friends, relatives, and neighbors that could help them survive—that would be a sign of abundance and hope? Perhaps we would fill our bags with forgiveness. How would it feel for someone you know to hand you a bag overflowing with forgiveness—not with large gestures or any strings attached, not even expecting a "Thank you"? How about a bag of trust and support? How about economic support and unlimited professional references during a time of transition between jobs? What if bags full of such things were exchanged naturally and casually, every time we came together—every time we hosted each other or a newcomer in our home, our workplace, or our church? I believe that is what God invites us to do. We are to be a people who generate, exchange, and live out of abundance.

Discussions about the Feeding of the Five Thousand tend pretty easily to get bogged down, to get caught on logistical or historical questions. Were there really five thousand people there? Did a bona fide miracle happen, or did people just start pulling their own stashes out of their knapsacks? Where, exactly, did this feeding occur? What kind of fish was served? I've even seen long, angry articles claiming that because we only know how many men were present, Matthew must not care about the women.

There is a place for these discussions, but I wonder why we fall into them so easily. I wonder whether we are afraid of the story—because if it's true, in any way you want to define *true*, then we might have to loosen our grip on those things we tend to keep stashed away in our fists, our bread boxes, and our hearts. If the story is in any sense true, then the part of it where Jesus turns to his disciples and says, "You give them something to eat," might just be the scariest part.

After all, it's usually easier to ask for forgiveness from an unseen God than to offer forgiveness to a very visible relative or coworker. Easier to ask God to help those in need than to take action that relieves suffering. Easier to speak of the "God of abundance" than to believe that we have skills, gifts, resources, and time to create abundance for others. "You give them something to eat," Jesus says. We swallow hard, and say, "It's just a story."

Paul asserts that "neither death, nor life, nor angels, nor rulers, nor things present, nor things to come, nor powers, nor height, nor depth, nor anything else in all creation, will be able to separate us from the love of God in Christ." Do you believe that? It is what we claim every time we come together here. It is why we stand and sit and kneel in these pews. It is the claim we wrap ourselves in when we emerge from the font at our baptism, and it will be the first thing proclaimed at our burial. What does that claim look like when we really live it?

It looks like a bunch of people sharing bread and fish on a hillside. It looks like a table set in the wilderness. It looks like a kiodo over-full with mangos and bananas, avocados and onions. It looks like the continuing exchange of forgiveness and hope, unconditional love, tears, and deep, deep laughter. There is no one right way to do this. There are an infinite number of ways to do this.

Nothing will separate us from the love of God. This is the ground of our freedom, the source of our abundance—an abundance a needy world desperately seeks. "You give them something to eat."

Amy McCreath is priest in charge, St. Christopher's Church,
River Hills, Wisconsin.

Present Your Bodies

Romans 12:1–8
Jennifer Phillips

EVERY SUNDAY in my college chapel, the chaplain, Lutheran pastor H. Paul Santmire, would come to the center aisle at the offertory and recite these words: "I call upon you, sisters and brothers, to present your bodies as a living sacrifice holy and acceptable to God, which is your spiritual worship. Do not be conformed to this world, but be transformed by the renewing of your minds, so that you may discern what is the will of God—what is good and acceptable and perfect."

Over the years, they soaked into me more and more, and I began to hear them clearly. Paul does *not* say, "Make your bodies into a living sacrifice that would be holy and acceptable to God." No. Paul says, "present your bodies as a living sacrifice"; in other words, your bodies, with all their life, as you offer them *already are* holy and acceptable to God. This word was incredibly important and powerful in a community of young women. Each in our own way carried with us the whisperings of our families, of Madison Avenue, of Hollywood, of Mattel Toys, and of our own fears and shame, that in some way our own newly adult female bodies were faulty, imperfect, dangerous, ugly, dirty, or needing to be fiercely controlled and reshaped toward some ideal that we suspected was impossible to achieve.

Our dorms, like those, I suspect, of many of you who were girls of the baby boomer generation, were full of young women on the latest fad diet or, in some extreme cases, bingeing in the cafeteria and throwing up in the bathroom. Or they were using cigarettes, or even amphetamines, to control weight, scorning the massive elastic undergarments of previous generations. And to those of us who went to listen and were able to hear, from our beloved male chaplain and the apostle Paul (not commonly seen as a friend to women's emancipation), week after week came this healing word: *your bodies, however they are today, are holy and acceptable to God.*

Last week, I caught the end of a public radio interview with a man whose special area of research is American boys. He was saying that today, adolescent boys are increasingly suffering from the same damaged body image—lack of esteem, manifestation of self-abusive eating disorders, and bodily manipulation by steroids, smoking, and dieting. He mentioned the *Baywatch* ideal of teen beauty—for both genders—which can only be accomplished by fortunate genetic inheritance with good health during a short span of years, and can *never* be fully accomplished by more than a tiny percentage of human beings, no matter how much effort we exert.

Paul says that the way it becomes possible for us imperfect, sinful creatures to present ourselves *in our bodies* before God, trusting that we are acceptable and holy, is by a transformation through the renewing of our minds. Was Paul an early proponent of cognitive therapy? Maybe. For he is certainly suggesting that, as we *think*, so shall we be *changed*. He goes on also to say that grace, the gift of God, is behind our transformation and renewal. We don't just get there by our own sheer willpower and determination. We don't get there by a diet. We don't get there by taking a drug. We don't get there just by being born lucky. We get to transformation, we get to the wisdom that allows us to discern the will of God, chiefly by "the mercies of God" to which we respond by presenting ourselves bodily as an offering to God.

Paul does not say, "Offer your spiritual self to God"—offer just the good part, just the part uncomplicated by sin, free of lust, gluttony, idleness, pride, sex, flab, and wrinkles. Paul says, "Offer your bodies in a self-giving, real way, and *this* action is your spiritual worship." Pretty amazing!

Paul goes on to warn us against the other extreme of grandiosity: "Don't think of yourself more highly than you ought to think." It took a couple of thousand years for psychologists to recognize that grandiosity, an overblown sense of self-importance, is really just another facet of the same fractured sense of self that those who judge themselves worthless, hateful, and ugly suffer. "Think with sober judgment," says Paul. Make a realistic self-assessment. Here, we need one another as the corrective to our sometimes distorted thoughts about ourselves. In the community, in the Body of Christ, we are diverse, and we have differing gifts, and not all members have the same *praxis* (the Greek word for "doing," "action"), the same ability to put things together in our lives, to see and act and think in a holistic way, congruently. By the transformation of our minds, we will learn the discipline, the discernment, the good sense to follow God's will as the bodily creatures we are. God will help; we are to collaborate, but we are not to wait until we have got it right to bring ourselves before God, hoping that we are *perfect*. There's nothing like middleaging to make clear just how we are *not* moving toward perfection! But what—God willing—we are moving toward is *maturity*, that other meaning of the Greek word *teleios*.

And so I put it to you that today, when I will insert Paul's words as that optional piece of our eucharistic worship, the Offertory Sentences, you open your hearts and minds to God's tender mercies. With full attention and trust, listen to the words of the Great Thanksgiving. Notice how we are reminded that "Christ our Passover is sacrificed for us"—that God does not need any bloody offering from us because of our sin, that God has already begun leading us into freedom in the new land of promise of God's reign, and that we are not to walk around thinking that we are trapped, enslaved, in chains.

Hear the invitation to you, in your body, to come forward and receive the fullness of God, as I say "The Gifts of God for the People of God"— which the Eastern church says even more explicitly are "Holy gifts for holy people." Get up out of your seat then and bring your body—your aging body, your plump body, your wrinkled body, your skinny body, your sick body, your aching body, your grief-pained body, your tired body, your healthy body, your lovely body, your *holy* body up here to the altar to be filled with Christ's Body. Offer yourself whole and living, just as you are, and know—keep telling yourself, if you need to; make it your mantra—that you are acceptable to God, in God's great mercy and love. God whispers to you, "Beloved, before you were conceived, I knew you; I loved you. I knit you together in your mother's womb. You are marvelously and awesomely made."

Jennifer Phillips is vicar of St. Augustine's Church, Kingston, Rhode Island.

PROPER TWENTY

Angry Enough to Die!

Jonah 3:10–4:11; Matthew 20:1–16
Sheila Nelson-McJilton

"JONAH, is it right for you to be angry?"

"Yes, angry enough to die!"

Jonah is not having a great day. In fact, Jonah hasn't had a great week. Jonah is at home, minding his own business, when God commands him to go to that great and evil city of Ninevah to preach repentance. Rather than obey, Jonah runs away to the port of Joppa. He gets on a boat and heads for Tarshish with a group of foreign sailors. A great storm arises, the sailors panic, Jonah "fesses up;" and in desperation, the sailors finally throw Jonah into the sea. Jonah spends three days and nights inside what Scripture calls "a great fish" that God sends to save him.

A second time, God commands Jonah to go to Ninevah and preach repentance. This time, he obeys. Reluctantly. You can almost see Jonah, dragging his feet, taking his sweet time on the road to Ninevah. Ninevah is one of the largest cities in the ancient world. In fact, it is so large, it takes a person three days to walk through it. And since Jonah is probably still dragging his feet, it looks as if he will spend more time in Ninevah than he did in that great fish.

On the first day, Jonah proclaims that if the people of Ninevah do not repent in forty days, they are history. To Jonah's amazement, when he is only one-third of the way through the city, the people listen to what he has to say. They believe his message. They declare a fast. Repent of their violence and evil ways. And God, whose love and mercy are much greater than God's anger, spares the people.

You might think Jonah would be happy now. He has been a reluctant prophet. But he has finally obeyed God and proclaimed God's message. Every person in Ninevah, from the greatest to the least, has turned from evil, and now worships God. But Jonah is not having a great day. He has survived being thrown into a raging sea, and survived three days and nights in the belly of a great fish. His life has been spared, and the Ninevites have all repented. Yet Jonah is angry. Angry enough to die. Why? Because Jonah and his people hate Ninevah.

Ninevah is part of the Assyrian Empire, an empire that has destroyed Israel. The Assyrian Empire is the Third Reich of the Ancient Near East. Jonah is angry because after he has obeyed God and preached destruction and good riddance to the Evil Empire, God has changed God's mind! And now, Jonah looks like a fool. "O LORD! is not this what I said while I was still in my own country? That is why I fled to Tarshish at the beginning; for I knew that you are a gracious God and merciful, slow to anger, and abounding in steadfast love, and ready to relent from punishing—See, God, I told you so. If you had just saved these stupid people from the get-go like I knew you would, I could have stayed home and avoided a lot of grief."

"Is it right for you to be angry?" God asks. Jonah does not answer God at all. Instead, once again, Jonah runs away. He goes out of Ninevah, makes a shelter, and sits under it to pout. If God finally sees Jonah's side and destroys these barbaric Ninevites, maybe he will see some fireworks after all.

God provides a growing bush to give Jonah shade from the scorching desert sun. But the next day, just when Jonah is enjoying the shade, a worm attacks the bush. It withers. Jonah is exposed, and angry again. A second time, God asks him about anger. "Is it right for you to be angry about the bush?"

"Yes, angry enough to die!"

That's pretty angry, Jonah. Anger is a destructive emotion. Sometimes anger is righteous anger. It can lead to needed changes. Jesus' anger about commercialism in the Temple—a house of prayer—led him to overturn tables. Thirty years ago in the United States, righteous anger about racial prejudice and injustice gave birth to the civil rights movement.

Jonah's anger, however, is not righteous anger. Jonah may feel compassion for a small group of foreign sailors and let them throw him overboard. He may feel compassion for a plant he did not grow. But Jonah does not feel compassion for a hundred twenty thousand people who repent and turn to God. Jonah seems to want God's love and mercy, but only on his own terms.

The laborers in the vineyard fall into this category as well. All of the laborers may be equal, but some want to be more equal than others. But God's math is not the same as ours. God's love and mercy are always greater than, not equal to or less than, human anger.

More often than not, the anger we see and experience seems to be greater than love and mercy. Every day, we experience the kind of selfish anger that leads to destruction. One day a man walked into a Baptist church in Fort Worth, Texas, shot seven innocent people to death, then killed himself. At whom was this man angry? We don't know. We know that he totally destroyed the inside of his own home. Then he destroyed the lives of seven innocent strangers. Then he destroyed his own life. All we know for sure is that, instead of love and mercy that give abundant life, selfish and distorted anger resulted in tragic death.

"Jonah, is it right for you to be angry?"

"Yes, angry enough to die."

In our own lives, we experience anger in ways that are subtle and yet just as destructive. We hold grudges against relatives or people with whom we work. We stubbornly refuse to forgive them. We resist allowing love and mercy to be greater than anger. We sit under our own bushes, pouting—watching people and events from afar to see what happens, hoping "they'll get theirs" for injustices and difficulties they have caused us. And we destroy no one but ourselves.

The evil Ninevites have repented, and so have their children and their animals. They can now live abundantly, in community and in right relationship with God. It is Jonah who pouts alone in the desert, with scorching sun and wind burning his face and his heart. Jonah's anger is destroying only Jonah.

Our anger, directed at other people, destroys only us. It may not destroy us physically—although it may. At the very least, when we allow anger in its many forms—jealousy, silence, depression, physical abuse, emotional abuse—to consume us, we allow anger to destroy us from the inside.

We really are in the same boat as is Jonah. And this is good news.

Good news? Why?

It is good news because of God. In this short book about a stubborn and reluctant prophet named Jonah, God shows just how generous divine love and mercy can be. A loving God pursues Jonah to teach him a lesson, and spares the lives of foreign sailors. God spares Jonah's life in the belly of a great fish. God spares the lives of Ninevites who repent of evil lives and turn to worship God. Finally, a loving God pursues Jonah once again.

Now, in the desert, God no longer commands Jonah to *do* anything. God asks pointed questions and lets Jonah come up with answers. This patient and merciful God is a gentle guide, asking Jonah to reflect upon the meaning and value of anger. Whether the issue is great—the fate of a hundred twenty thousand men, women, and children—or small—the withering of a little bush in the desert, God allows Jonah to figure out that anger is a destructive emotion.

When we are angry, our fury says much more about the one who is angry than about the objects of that anger. This is true when we are angry at people who look or act differently than we do, or who hold different political or theological views from us. This is true when we hold grudges against family members or coworkers. This is true when we internalize anger so much that we alienate someone by cold silence, or when we hit them, or when we speak harshly to them. For anger is just as destructive to those around us in a thousand daily ways as it is when innocent people are shot in cold blood by an angry man.

But God's divine love and mercy are far greater than our human anger, and God is willing to wait for us and to guide us in figuring this out. God knows the end of the story, that story full of divine love and mercy, and through eternity, love and mercy will continue to be greater than our human, selfish, destructive anger.

As Christians, we have the ability to experience even more of this divine love and mercy than Jonah could, centuries before Jesus Christ walked among us on this earth. We can read the book of Jonah and hear God ask, "Jonah, do you have a right to be angry?"

We can hear Jonah reply, "Yes, angry enough to die."

And because we know the greater story, we can almost hear Jonah, or ourselves, ask, "God, do you have a right to be angry with me?"

And we can hear God reply, "Yes, I have a right to be angry with you. But my love and mercy are far greater than my anger. I love you. In fact, I love you enough to die on a cross. And in dying, I love you enough to give you MY abundant and eternal life."

Sheila Nelson-McJilton is assistant rector of Christ Church, Stevensville, Maryland.

PROPER TWENTY-FIVE

We Are What God Calls Us

Matthew 22:34–46
Margaret Ann Faeth

RALPH WALDO EMERSON used to greet old friends with the question, "What has become clear to you since we last met?" It is an intriguing question, isn't it? I had always assumed that, as I got older or more educated, life would become clearer to me—that I would be able to answer some of the big questions. And happily, in a few cases that has been true. I have learned that my life seems to make more sense when I organize my time and energy around the things that matter the most—my God, my marriage, my family, my friends, and my vocation. I have learned that I cannot possibly please all of the people all of the time, and that integrity is more important than popularity. I have learned that if I don't take care of myself, then there is little left to offer in service to others.

But I'll be the first to admit that the more I learn, the more I realize how little I know. Many of life's mysteries, big and small, still elude me. I still haven't figured out how to separate the whisperings of the Spirit from the other noises inside my soul. I haven't figured out how to fit all the things I would like to do into a twenty-four-hour day. I'm still not very good at letting God be in charge of the agenda and the schedule. And I'm still baffled by the mystery of what happens to the socks that disappear in the wash, although one of my professors, a wise man indeed, insists that those lost socks are somehow transformed into hangers and end up in our closets.

What has become clear to you since we last met? I wonder what the Pharisees would answer if we asked them that question after their encounter with Jesus? They might well say, "Nothing!" It seems obvious from the test they pose that the Pharisees go to Jesus not to learn but to trap him. "When the Pharisees heard that [Jesus] had silenced the Sadducees, they gathered together, and one of them, a lawyer, asked him a question to test him. 'Teacher, which commandment is the greatest?'" Matthew makes the context of this question very clear. First of all, Matthew is careful to specify that it is a lawyer who asks the question. This man, representing the Pharisees, comes to Jesus as one who thinks he already knows the answer to the question he is asking. The lawyer calls Jesus "Teacher" instead of "Lord." This man is not a believer. This question is a test. In Matthew's Gospel, the only ones who test Jesus are Satan and the Pharisees. Matthew's version is very different from the story in Mark, where a sincere believer asks Jesus the same question. Matthew has set up an adversarial situation where unbelief encounters the truth of the gospel.

The lawyer knew that the Hebrew interpretation of Scripture put all the law on equal footing. The minutiae of the dietary law were as important as the major themes of charity and forgiveness. To presume to rank the laws according to importance was to assume the prerogatives of God. So to ask Jesus which of the commandments was the greatest was to ask Jesus if he dared to do what the law and the prophets dared not do—to speak with the authority of God. And so he did. "'You shall love the Lord your God with all your heart, and with all your soul, and with all your mind,'" Jesus says. "This is the greatest and first commandment. And a second is like it: 'You shall love your neighbor as yourself.' On these two commandments hang all the law and the prophets." The story ends with the observation that from then on, no one dared to put Jesus to the test.

I suppose we all get some satisfaction out of the stories where Jesus outwits those who set out to trick him, but to leave such stories simply as an expression of Jesus' cleverness would be to miss the point. Jesus' response invites us to see the truth. The law and the prophets are to be understood in the light of love. Jesus' clever response is not an act of one-upmanship. It is an invitation to a new way of seeing things. It is an invitation to learning and growth. It is the startling revelation that loving God is inextricably linked with loving our neighbor. Perhaps it is in some sense a warning that loving God and neighbor is far more than a commandment, it is a way of life.

In his book *Life on the Mississippi*, Mark Twain wrote of the life of the riverboat captains. In admiration, he observed: "Two things seemed pretty apparent to me. One was that to be a river pilot a man had got to learn more than any one man ought to be allowed to know; and the other was, that he must learn it all over again in a different way every twenty-four hours."[1] Loving God and our neighbor is even more complex than piloting a riverboat. There are hidden dangers and new challenges at every bend. Sometimes those we love disappoint us. Sometimes they just won't love us back the way we want to be loved. And sometimes those we are called to love are so flawed that they seem completely unlovable.

I know that some of you are probably following major league baseball as the season comes to its climax. And I suppose that some of you share my habit of doing a little bit of armchair umpiring. But before we get too hot and bothered about bad calls, it is important to remember that we can't see things the same way the umpire behind the plate sees them. I heard of three umpires who were reflecting on the process of calling the game. "I call them as I see them," the first umpire said. "I call them as they are," answered the second. Finally, the wisest of the three responded, "They ain't nothing UNTIL I call them."

I think that is the point of this Gospel. We are what God calls us to be. God loves the unlovable because he sees us not only our flaws but also our beauty and potential. When God looks at you and at me, he sees channels of grace—lives through which his own love can be expressed to the world. That is why the law of love, as Jesus summarizes it for us, demands that we stop judging and start loving one another. Alfred North Whitehead once said, "Seek simplicity, and then distrust it." Loving each other is far more easily said than done.

What is becoming clear here? I think it is that Jesus offers a new way of seeing things—a way to navigate the journey of life and love. Jesus reminds us that clarity in this life comes not from our skill, but through God's mercy and grace. The demands of the law and the proclamation of the prophets seem random and capricious without the light of love. Jesus can speak with authority because he is the incarnate Word, the very embodiment of God's loving and creative truth. In the light of the cross we can see just how costly this love can be. And in the light of Easter, we can see just how much love can accomplish.

As Christians, our clarity comes in our regular encounters with the risen Christ—in scripture and sacrament and prayer. Our encounters with the Lord are invitations to look beyond the set of rules that govern our own lives and to bring the larger themes into focus. What good does it do us to go to the right schools, live in the right neighborhoods, and associate with the right kinds of people if we are spiritually impoverished? What good is it to gain the whole world but lose our souls in the process?

Warren Bennis, the management expert, makes an important distinction between behaviors that we undertake to prove ourselves and behaviors we engage in to express ourselves. We prove ourselves out of fear, we express ourselves out of gratitude. *Proving* limits us to asking the questions to which we already have decided the answers. *Expressing* ourselves lets us look for those rare glimpses of clarity amidst the ambiguities of life. *Proving* forces us into competition; *expressing* invites us into cooperation.

The summary of the law, our baptismal promises, and our covenant with one another as members of a community of faith all call us to lay aside the burden of proving ourselves and take on the challenge of expressing our confidence in, and gratitude for, God's love for us.

In our encounters with Christ, it becomes clear that the more we know about the mystery of love, the more we need to learn. But we come to Christ willing to listen and learn, ready to be changed and challenged by the encounter. In the end, we are what God calls us.

Margaret Ann Faeth is associate rector of Immanuel Church on the Hill, Alexandria, Virginia.

---

1. Mark Twain, *Life on the Mississippi* (New York, Bantam Books, 1981), p. 41.

PROPER TWENTY-SEVEN

The Bridegroom's Light

Amos 5:18–24; Matthew 25:1–13
John T. Koenig

SOME OF you will know that the author Frederick Buechner, a Presbyterian minister trained uptown at Union Theological Seminary, made his mark as a popular theologian with a quartet of novels about the improbable Leo Bebb, a Christian evangelist and con artist. With the Bebb novels, I suspect, Buechner is wanting to tell us something about all Christian evangelists—not just the kind we laugh at when we see them on television, but also those who worship and evangelize in a more refined manner, namely, us. The narrator of all four novels and, besides Bebb, chief protagonist, is Antonio Parr, a rather aimless and passive young man who is trying to be a writer, but not doing very well at it. Antonio has a twin sister, Miriam, who, in the first novel, is dying of bone cancer.

Miriam is a tough lady, a lapsed Catholic agnostic, a chain-smoker and sipper of martinis right up to the end. When Antonio sees her alive for the last time, he is shepherding his nephew, Miriam's son, because Miriam's ex-husband, who usually takes care of the boy, has skipped town. The boy is also named Tony, after his uncle. At this sad, sad leave-taking (and they all know it is the last), Miriam confers a kind of benediction on her son. "Tony," she says, "just keep your eyes open and stay awake." Antonio the elder is startled because he knows his sister's words are meant for him, too. "Tony, stay awake. Stay alive—really alive." Throughout the four novels, in dreams and memories, these last words of Miriam come back to haunt Antonio. "Stay awake, Antonio. You haven't got as much time as you think. Live now. Live authentically."

"Keep awake therefore, for you know neither the day nor the hour." I wonder if Buechner's entire quartet of novels about Leo Bebb isn't a kind of arabesque on these words of Jesus, with Miriam in the role of Christ. Like the scene in Miriam's hospital room, the parable of the ten bridesmaids that precedes these famous words doesn't bring us much comfort. It has to do with what we now call the second coming of Christ, a difficult doctrine, to say the least. It has to do with a final division between the wise and foolish, and with the latter's exclusion from the messianic marriage feast. "Lord, Lord, open to us," they cry. But he replies: "Truly I tell you, I do not know you." Harsh words. Can this be the Jesus who eats with tax collectors and sinners, the Good Shepherd who leaves the flock to search out the one lost sheep? And tonight, Amos compounds our trouble by reminding us that the Day of the Lord could turn out to be not at all what we desire.

How can we let this stern message from Scripture (by no means an isolated one) work on us without becoming disheartened, without getting our gospel hope snuffed out? Maybe we should look first at what has become so odd to us about the parable, at that firm conviction among the earliest believers that Jesus would return to them soon, visibly, even in their lifetime, to host them at the messianic banquet. This teaching, as we all know, has led to some pretty bizarre behavior in the church. And as the new millennium dawns, we're likely to witness a lot more of it. But the point of the parable, and of many sayings like it in the New Testament, is that we cannot know, cannot predict, cannot calculate the final moment of our world's ordinary history. "But about that day or hour no one knows, neither the angels in heaven, nor the Son, but only the Father." Not even Jesus had access to the heavenly timetable—which makes it highly unlikely that God's plans for humanity will reach their fulfillment at any particular time that anyone happens to designate. However, as to the next day . . .

Just as death catches us up short, just as death interferes so decisively with our plans, so will the day of the Lord. Everyone's work and play and joy will come out unfinished. The only thing to do then, and it's a wonderful thing, is to listen to Miriam, and to live each day fully alive, with as much authenticity and honesty and thanksgiving as we can muster. The folks in Alcoholics Anonymous have learned this very Christian lesson: one day at a time. Every moment is precious—a gift from God.

Another thing about the prospect of the second coming is that it shows us how ends and goals and outcomes of projects, no matter how noble they may appear to us, can never justify inhumane means. When our life gets interrupted for the last time, with everything still unfinished, we will be told in no uncertain terms how we come out on this one. Did we treat the people we got to know as useful tools for accomplishing our grand aims, or as sisters and brothers for whom Christ died? Being an administrator, I know that balancing ends and means, even with the best of intentions, can be daunting. Bishops and other public leaders have to do it every day. And so do we all. Yet the struggle itself is salutary, because gradually we learn to see each moment of decision making in the light of Christ's nearness, and therefore infused with grace.

Which brings us to another major theme in our parable: preparedness. On the surface of Jesus' story, some people seem good: the five wise bridesmaids who are well prepared, having brought along extra oil. But five other people appear less than good: the foolish bridesmaids, ill prepared because they have failed to stock their Y2K provisions. So, when the bridegroom comes (late by everyone's standards), the so-called foolish types panic. The oil has run low in their lamps. First they try to beg some, and when that doesn't work, they rush off to buy some more on the advice of their wise sisters. Finally (and tragically), they get shut out of the wedding feast—presumably because they are late in returning, although the bridegroom's rebuke to them doesn't quite fit that line of interpretation.

This inconsistency and other details of the story lead me to suspect that there's something more than the obvious going on here. When we think about it a little, we have to admit that none of the ten wedding attendants is really prepared to meet the bridegroom who is Christ. They've all fallen asleep, as humans must, and the five provident ones are not very virtuous about sharing their reserves. Maybe they weren't present at the Sermon on the Mount, or the feeding of the five thousand.

Here is where I feel personally most gripped by the parable. I probably fit into the wise bridesmaid category. Like many of the ordained, and those heading for ordination, I am a firstborn. We (along with single children) are overrepresented in grad schools, especially those connected with the church. We are the Eagle Scout types—the responsible ones, always prepared. (I never got close to Eagle, but I got the message.) Unfortunately, along with that "preparedness" mind-set comes another, less attractive one. We elder brothers and sisters tend to look at our younger siblings and friends with a certain haughtiness, an unspoken assumption that they will probably not get their act together unless we come to their aid. So we gravitate into the so-called helping professions. And we're pretty good at them, as long as we're not ruled by the dark side of our motivation.

"Give us some of your oil, for our lamps are going out." But the wise replied "No!" (the Greek is very strong: "*No way!*"). "There will not be enough for you and for us; you had better go to the dealers and buy some for yourselves." Great advice. Remember, it's midnight. Here is the cruelty of the competent coming out. And, of course, the fear. There will not be enough oil. "Do you want all of us to look stupid in front of the bridegroom when every lamp goes out early? No way!"

Well, these wise bridesmaids get into the wedding feast. But I wonder how they feel about their sisters' being excluded. And I wonder (if the bridegroom was, indeed, Jesus) what he said to them about their lack of generosity. Could they really celebrate?

Our parable ends on a note of heaviness. "I do not know you. . . ." I have to wonder if Jesus, now the risen Christ, does not want us to question his own telling of this story, especially its rigid divisions into "wise" and "foolish," and its portrait of the excluding bridegroom. Are we not led by the authority of the gospel itself at least to imagine an alternative ending to the story?

I think that, because of who Jesus is for us now, we not only *can* but *must* do so. Our reimaging shouldn't remove all the warnings contained in the story. Judgment is an integral part of the biblical message: We will be held accountable. But the way we are judged now, and will be judged on the last day, is likely to be far more mysterious than this parable implies.

How might the parable end differently, starting from the scene at midnight? We have to keep the sleep bit. We all fall asleep on the job. And the bridegroom does tarry, almost daring us to disbelieve in his advent. But what happens when he does finally arrive? The less than-prepared-bridesmaids still panic, and *some* of them plead with their sisters for more oil, a plea that is met, surprisingly, with a positive response from *some* of the so-called wise (who nevertheless hold on to their fear that there isn't going to be enough and everything will turn out badly at the feast).

But other members of the not-prepared contingent decide not to plead. Instead, they say out loud: "We could rush off to the stores and wake up the shopkeepers. But, you know, the really important thing is to stay here and greet the bridegroom, oil or not. We'll just have to say we're sorry if our lamps go out and rely on his good graces. We've got to assume he's in a good mood on his wedding night." At this, the other wise sisters, the ones who haven't shared their oil, experience a burning sensation in their chests, and are able to admit, still with some grumbling, that yes, maybe these younger ones are right and that they, the wise elders, probably put too much stock in duty and not enough in joy. So off they all go to meet the bridegroom, in diverse states of preparedness and all of them more than a little humbled. No a bad model for a typical service of Christian worship.

What will the bridegroom do? He will say: "You're all kind of foolish and you're all culpable. We'll talk about that in good time. But truly I tell you, I am glad to see each one of you. Come with me into the banquet hall, and together we'll figure out how to keep the place lit. After all, I am the light of the world."

Is this alternative ending pure fantasy on our parts, just wish fulfillment posing as hermeneutics? I don't think so. In the always-surprising letter to the Ephesians we find a little snippet of an early Christian hymn that goes like this: "Sleeper awake! Rise from the dead, and Christ will shine upon you." From the verses that surround the hymn we learn that the writer doesn't think of rising from the dead here as the final resurrection on the last day, but rather as our waking up from, our repentance from, the sins that beset us in our present life. Christ alone can provide the light for this awakening. To me, its seems likely that the author of Ephesians knew some version of tonight's parable and gave it an interpretation not so very different from the one we have spun out.

Stay awake, Antonio. Live authentically. Stay awake, John and Martha and Agnes. But even if you fall asleep, if you fall into inauthenticity and unpreparedness and false pride and fear—and you will—even then, know that your Lord seeks you out to rouse you with his light, to refashion your flickering lamp into a strong, clear beacon. One of the places where Christ does this most regularly is the meal called Eucharist we are about to celebrate, the foretaste of the wedding banquet he longs to share with us in the fullness of the Kingdom. "Come, my Light, my Feast, my Strength: such a light as shows a feast; such a feast as mends in length; such a strength as makes his guest." Well prayed, George Herbert. Let's go to meet this incomparable Bridegroom.

John T. Koenig is sub-dean for academic affairs and professor of New Testament at the General Theological Seminary in New York City.

PROPER TWENTY-EIGHT

We Are Kin

Zephaniah 1:7, 12–18; Matthew 25:14–15, 19–29
Judith Whelchel

AFTER LEAVING graduate school in social work, I went to Milledgeville, Georgia to work with abused children. Families there live in old farm sheds without plumbing or electricity. There are no clothes closets or free meals or flu shots. The place is, quite honestly, one in which it was easy for me to feel important—so much to be done, so many needy people.

Milledgeville was home to a child named Anna. She was beautiful—rosy dark skin and piercing black eyes, coupled with a smile that consumed, first her face, and then the room she inhabited. Her parents were crack cocaine addicts. Anna was one of seven children, all of whom were in foster care. Parental rights had been terminated, and Anna had been placed for adoption in a home with another four-year-old girl. After several months the foster family chose to adopt the other child, leaving Anna somehow doubly orphaned. Milledgeville is a small town. Anna would see her biological mother walking down the sidewalk, and scream from the bus, "MAMA, please come get me!"

Each week at the mental health center Anna would crawl her little body up next to me on the sofa, and we would read a story together. Usually she would then hop off the sofa and move on to the sand play, the dollhouse, or the art supplies. But one day she stayed curled up under my arm on the sofa. "Anna, are you ready to play?" I coaxed. She shook her head.

"It is good to be held for awhile," I offered.

She responded: "You are gonna have to hold me for my whole life."

I had been attracted to that place because there was so much for me to do. Six months into the deal, this little injured bird told me I could do nothing to remove the deep hole of her trauma. The question Anna carried was whether I could endure holding some part of her wound. I walked from the encounter, knowing that I was smaller than I had presumed—that my mission was simpler than I had imagined. And that our communal need for God, and for one another, is large indeed.

We do not take our life journey without the support of many others. Yet we are often unaware of our dependence upon each other. We are taught to be self-made, rugged individuals. People actually drive cars with bumper stickers proclaiming THE ONE WHO DIES WITH THE MOST TOYS WINS. That, of course is a big lie—and an old one.

Zephaniah warned Israel almost seven hundred years before the birth of Christ: "Though they build houses, they shall not inhabit them. Though they plant vineyards, they shall not drink wine from them." What matters is not the house or how it is appointed, the size of the vineyard or the quality of the grapes, but the importance of *being*—in our own bodies—homes, vessels, containers, *holders*.

The master in Matthew's parable disrupts our pride in rugged individualism. From the start he is keenly aware that we never take a journey without the support of those around us. Going on a journey, he leaves the hard work of maintaining his property, his wealth, to three servants. When he returns, two of his servants have done well, increasing the earnings of his fortune. They receive his blessing. The third servant adds nothing to the fortune of the master. He sits on what he has been given. He makes nothing for himself or his master. He shows no ingenuity, no creativity, no imagination. With what he has been entrusted, he maintains the status quo, refusing to dream, refusing to believe in anything fuller. Like the fluffy ostrich, he sticks his head in the sand.

Jesus, in telling this story, makes a point about how our lives fit into God's created order. Jesus—the vagabond, ragamuffin healer and evangelist, who was born to poor parents in a barn, who named tax collectors and lepers as his best friends, who turned over the money changers' tables in the Temple, who taught that we should share not just our shirts but our coats as well—*that* Jesus is *not* using this story to illustrate the importance of having our financial portfolios in order. Jesus couldn't care less about your portfolio, or my stuff.

The master is outraged at the apathy and stagnant imagination in his third servant. Jesus is calling his people to be visionaries, artists of creation— to dream, believe, imagine, be alive in our bodies. With the little piece of God's creation, with the resources that have been given us in trust— make good on the investment. Enlarge it. Think big and boldly. Take a risk. Play magician. The One to whom it all belongs is going to want to know what we have done with all our gifts.

In the same town of Milledgeville, I worked alongside a woman named Frances Veal. The Veals had lived in that part of Georgia since the middle of the last century. My coworker's ancestors had been plantation slaves. In the county there are Caucasian Veals and African-American Veals. Plantation life was such that slave women sometimes bore the children of their Caucasian owners. Stripped of the identity they brought with them from across the world, slaves were often given the name of the plantation family that claimed ownership of them.

Reginald Veal was a Caucasian child who came to the mental health center. Frances Veal and I stood talking one day in the waiting area. Someone walked out of the building, hollering over their shoulder, "Bye, Miss Veal!"

Little Reginald, also in the waiting area, piped up. "Is your name Veal?" he asked Francis.

"Last time I checked," Frances teased.

"My name is Veal, too!" Reginald exclaimed. "Miss Veal, we kin!"

Of course he is right. We are kin. What happens to you affects me. The choices you make with your life affect much more than your particular corner of the world. How we live in this country is manifest in the lives of people worlds away, whom we will never meet. What the servants do with the master's resources matters.

Judith Whelchel is vicar of the Church of the Advocate,
Asheville, North Carolina.

■ 4

Multicultural Issues in Preaching

Katharine Jefferts Schori

ANGLICANS HAVE long understood three sources of authority—scripture, tradition, and reason, to which a fourth source is often added—experience. Experience has been understood as a component of reason, or as a component of all three sources. These reflections begin from experience, and seek to address three primary issues: *who* preaches; *what* is preached, and *how* it is preached, exploring these issues in a variety of cultural settings.

Who Preaches?

Preaching in a cross-cultural setting is intrinsically prophetic, not only in the sense that "normal" preaching is or can be prophetic, but in the implicit challenge facing the preacher as the stranger in a strange land. The preacher's ability to be prophetic comes from the ability and willingness to stand in a liminal place relative to a community—neither to be wholly outside the community (and therefore with no real connection), nor to be so wholly identified with that community that no perspective is possible. The preacher who enters another cultural community as *gringa*, *haole*, honky, or *pakeha*, presents an affront by her very presence. The outsider as preacher will be heard very differently than an insider. Whence comes that liminal authority to be heard as preacher?

I work routinely in one cross-cultural context, and periodically in several others. I have primary responsibility for a small Spanish-speaking congregation sheltered in a much larger Anglo one. Week in and week out, the challenge is to preach subversive Good News to a congregation that initially sees me as a fully coopted member of the dominant and oppressive majority culture. At times it feels like God is sending Pharoah's minister to foment rebellion among the Hebrew slaves. Trust is the initial and major issue. The authority to preach is intimately connected with trust; and ordination (or licensing) does not necessarily bestow it. Authority is a significant issue in cultures that value the experience of elders and/or the patriarchal voice. The preacher who does not fit those traditional expectations provides a visual affront even before she or he begins to speak.

Another context in which I work occasionally is a Native one—the First Nations people of North America (sometimes overlapping the Hispanic one). First Nations peoples of the United States and Canada may use English in culturally mixed gatherings, but that doesn't mean we immigrants know what's going on. At the beginning of my work, I sat in on a cross-cultural pastoral care course, asking an occasional question, and participating in a fairly reserved way. A Native student with whom I work later told me, very diplomatically, that my behavior was offensive. I had no authority to speak there. Only elders were expected to raise questions and challenges.

In this Native context, and many others, the ability to "be heard" is not a function of office or ordination; it is a gift of the community to recognized elders. The preacher's task may be to hold council with the elders, allowing the gospel message to be shaped by that encounter, or challenging the elders themselves to preach the Good News.

A third context is the state university, where I occasionally teach religious studies. This is the technical state school—the one with veterinary medicine, agriculture, forestry, engineering, and oceanography programs. In recent decades it has had a decidedly anti-Christian or antireligious ethos, despite the presence of an excellent religious studies department (now consolidated with the philosophy department). Most of the currently visible Christian presence on campus is of the highly fundamentalist stripe. Some students, however, are beginning to ask for more.

A course I taught on world views in the Bible had a small, vocal group of fundamentalist students. Class discussions occasionally deteriorated into debates about the validity of a scholarly approach to the Bible. After one such discussion continued into the hall after class, I said to one student: "You must find this class extremely frustrating."

"Oh, no," he responded, "my spiritual armor is much stronger now than it was before the class began."

My point is that authority is an issue even here. Part of my role as professor is to invite students to broaden understandings, to ask more questions, even to invite doubt about fondly held positions—in general, to stimulate their thought processes. As an Anglican Christian, my task is to do all of this in a way that invites the possibility of hearing good news. There are days when it feels akin to being thrown into the arena, albeit one in which the animals seem to be fellow Christians. Good news may be preached as much in how one approaches the conflict as in any words that are said.

Yet another context is the pastoral work I do as a hospice chaplain. The calling is to provide pastoral care and spiritual support to the dying and their families—people of all faith traditions, and none. The greatest challenge is to invite people to reflect on their relationship with the sacred, or "something more," when they have no formal religious background, or are actively hostile to religion. An attitude of apathy, even hostility toward religion is almost a cultural norm in the western and northwestern United States.

This hospice provides an annual service of remembrance in which loved ones who have died in the last year are recalled by name. We listen to some quiet music, and gather for refreshments afterward. The chaplain's task is to give "the message"—to preach good news in consciously nonreligious but spiritually authentic language. The ability to be heard in this context depends on one's willingness to enter into the thought world of this non-religious culture, and invite the possibility of a different and larger understanding.

A final context has to do with the diversity of congregational life within one not-so-large diocese. We have a growing number of churches that don't have the traditional model of one fulltime, seminary-trained priest, that have seldom been served that way, and that cannot look to that model. These congregations live in the midst of a dominant church culture (the megachurch model, as well as large Episcopal churches) that tells them they are failures. My task in working with them is to speak truth about the reality of their situations, and to celebrate the creative ministry that is happening in each congregation. The authority to speak good news comes from entering into the world of each worshipping community, valuing its unique gifts, and preaching the Good News that new life is possible, even in the face of death.

What Do We Preach?

Liberation theologians have taught us that good news depends on one's perspective. To preach the virtues of voluntary simplicity is probably entirely appropriate in a wealthy suburban congregation; but it may not be good news to families of six or eight who live in two-bedroom apartments and struggle to keep their children fed and clothed. The indignity of poverty is supposed to lead to indignation, and to the overturning of social systems that divide and oppress God's people. The task in preaching to the poor I know is not to encourage faith in God—which they seem to have in abundance—but to invite a vision of something that looks more like God's banquet table. The prophetic challenge is to confront fatalism and say, "Don't lie down in Egypt and die. Don't let Pharoah suck your lifeblood—you who labor from dawn to dusk for unjust wages. God is with you now, yes; but God is also with us in the battle for justice."

How Do We Preach?

I call this work of multicultural preaching my "ministry of incompetence." I have a friend, a former Jesuit, who talks about the third degree of humility—being willing to make an abject fool of one's self for the sake of the gospel. The reality is that someone without traditional authority, with limited language skills and imperfect knowledge of the culture, can't possibly preach an eloquent sermon. I have long since thrown out the laboriously translated Spanish version of the day's English sermon, although I note that sometimes a loose version of the children's sermon works better than anything else. I've wrestled with whether story, image, or thesis works best in preaching in another cultural context. I'm not sure there is an answer.

How do I preach? In the Spanish-language context, *naked*—no text, no pulpit, inadequate ability to conjugate, and limited vocabulary. Once, at Easter, I so offended one of the congregation by talking about the Resurrection as God's cosmic joke that he got up and walked out. But God is gracious. That man is now one of the most committed members of this congregation.

Sometimes the very resources we expect will liberate—the stories of God's people delivered—only serve to tighten the chains. The most readily available Spanish translation of the Bible becomes a subtle political document, when texts that speak of awe at the divine presence, or humility in meeting Jesus, are routinely couched in terms of abject unworthiness and abasement. The texts of terror in this culture are ones that serve to cement colonial chains. Exegeting the community, reading the oral newspaper of daily living, is at least as important in preaching in a different cultural context, but it is far harder to do when one doesn't know how to read the subtleties, or the subtitles.

The cultural issues I've pointed to may seem larger or more extreme than what most Anglos regularly wrestle with. But I want to encourage us to think about the different cultures operating in the spheres wherein we work. The 8 A.M. congregation has a significantly different culture from the 9 A.M. or the 11:15 congregation. The 8 A.M. congregation I preach to uses Rite I and like to arise early, get church over with quickly, and avoid too much music. Many are politically conservative. Few are under the age of sixty. Yet many are people of deep, if private, faith. I see the task in that culture as expanding social consciousness, pushing the comfort zone, yet speaking comfort to those who are aging and, in the sight of the world, declining.

Every preacher is faced with a variety of cultural contexts. If we're willing to begin exploring them, we will find the preaching experience both more challenging and more rewarding. Willingness to walk into what we may see as the lion's den of another culture will be an important witness in and of itself. And the conversation with the lion may turn out to be a two-way hearing of good news.

Katharine Jefferts Schori has recently taken office as the bishop of Nevada. When this article was written, she was serving in a number of pastoral capacities in the Diocese of Oregon.

Surviving the Sermon Preparation Process

Eugene L. Lowry

PREACHING A sermon is relatively easy. Preparing one worth preaching is difficult. Like Elijah in the cave, we wait for the divine voice. We look everywhere for the Word. Often, the more we look the less we find. Through the years I have been given advice at great length—told where to look for sermon possibilities: through disciplined Bible study, in my pastoral experience, on my knees, at the theater, in the paper, in my lying down and my rising up. Of course, we have the lectionary—look there.

But the problem remains, for, alas, the issue is not *where*—but *what*. Would we be instructed by the P.S. attached to the bottom of that very old recipe for rabbit soup: "First, you catch a rabbit"? Partly, but unfortunately that advice won't suffice either. The issue is not simply catching the homiletical rabbit, but whether you can *intentionally* and *inadvertently* allow the rabbit to catch you. That is what this essay is about—how to allow the homiletical rabbit to *catch us.*

I venture this in spite of my long-held suspicion that most folks who tell others how to get started in the sermon preparation process either do not really know how they do it, or do not seem to follow their own advice. The issue is, after all, the most elusive part of the homiletical art—and clearly the hardest to teach. Most of us know several options regarding the shaping of a sermon—*if only we had something to shape.*

You remember that moment, when someone close to you steps into the middle of your sermon preparation with: "How are you doing for Sunday?"

You respond: "Not well. Nothing seems to be happening."

Later the person returns with the same question—and out of an entirely different world you exclaim: "I think I have something!" (It probably would be more accurate to say that something *has you.*)

But the inquirer is not content—wants more: "What is it that you have?"

Your initial reaction is to ask the person to leave, and quickly—because your only honest reply would be, "I don't really know yet, but something *is working*."

Our question, then, is: How does one prompt, tease, evoke, claim, provoke, or facilitate that uncertain certainty—"I think I have something"? Actually, we will take the matter one step further, asking—once we arrive at that moment—How can we keep alive that almost euphoric epistemological experience before it turns to pale platitude? How do we live with it in the context of further preparation? We will presume that the preacher begins with a text—lectionary or otherwise. The preparation process begins, obviously, by gaining an effective familiarity with the text to be utilized. Otherwise form will not follow function. This "effective familiarity" involves a peculiar blend of knowledge and mystery, of grasping and being grasped, of managing and being led. It is easier to say what it is not than what it is—although most of us know when it is happening well.

Numerous traps await the preacher in the preparation process—traps that hide homiletical rabbits and often prevent those preliminary "Ah Ha!" experiences that forecast productive homiletical work. In the process of exploring several traps to be avoided we will attempt also to identify techniques that might prove helpful in successfully surviving the preparation process.

Because the first task is to listen to the text, it is important not to be upstaged by expert helpers who will give us answers to questions we have yet to ask. I believe too many preachers (lectionary followers in particular) turn much too quickly from a first reading of the text to brief commentaries so easily available. I am not quarreling with exegetical assistance. Indeed, without it, text turns to pre-text, and what might have been biblical preaching turns into manipulative topical preaching. Exegetical assistance is an indispensable part of biblical preaching. But its time is not now.

Since our first task is hearing, it is important to position ourselves in such a way that we can be open to listening. Our intention to "get a sermon" is commendable—and inevitable, for Sunday is fast approaching. Yet, our task at this early moment in the preparation process should be to set aside our intentionality in favor of that possibility of inadvertent surprise. We already have enough trouble with imposing our own agenda onto a text. Right now, let's not impose others' agendas either. Instead, I suggest we read the text out loud, repeatedly—and in as many differing translations and paraphrases as we have available. It is particularly helpful to read the text in the original language if possible—not yet for purposes of exegetical scrutiny, but for the purpose of hearing. I suggest delaying word study at this point—unless something jumps out and slaps us in the face. Right now we are trying to be impacted by the whole. Dissecting the parts will come later. At this moment we need to find behavior that will keep us out of the driver's seat. Our present concern is to be accosted, confronted. Does this mean that all we can do is to wait around, prayerfully and quietly, for the Word to drop by? I think not.

There is something we can do that by its nature can help keep us out of the driver's seat and assist the possibility of our being confronted. *We can look for trouble.* What is there about the text that does not seem to fit? Is there anything strange here? "Ideological suspicion" does not always feel comfortable for us—particularly when we are included in its object. But suspicion in its positive sense of probing uncertainty is precisely what can be helpful. Trouble in, around, with, and about the text is often the occasion for a fresh hearing. In lectionary workshops, I often ask the participants to gather in small groups and look for what is weird in a passage. Anything is helpful if it breaks us loose from the usual, the easily accepted, the routine and timid truth that will not change lives. Sometimes the "trouble" will not show itself until we have read the previous two chapters of the text—and the following chapter as well. Our particular text, after all, did not come out of a vacuum. Its placement in the biblical sweep was the result of someone's conscious strategy. We are looking for trouble, for textual issues. As we are confronted by them, we then begin—like any good detective—to research them. But, looking for trouble needs to come first.

After textual issues begin to be named, then such measures as word study, introductions to the book as found in commentaries, comparisons with parallel or conflicting passages—all the resources of solid exegetical work—are in order. Now we are on the kind of trail for disclosure that has life and vitality. But, note the difference between exploring a text to find its *answer* and exploring a text to pursue its *question*. The first puts us in command. The second, while prompting similar exegetical work, positions us as investigator rather than as explainer. Instead of placing us in a nice tidy little circle with God and the text as over against the listeners, we become the first listener.

In all of this we are headed toward the first major moment in the sermon preparation process, which is to answer the question: *What is the focus of the text?* The question of focus is born out of the need to know what is at stake here, what were the biblical issues that needed to be addressed in the first place. Sometimes the biblical text does not appear to name a specific issue, but rather contains a fairly straight forward declaration of some kind, which means the preacher needs to look before and after the specific text in order to find the focus—or, perhaps, imaginatively to the anticipated reaction of the original receivers, or even next Sunday's congregation.

When the preacher's early preparation work on a sermon concentrates on focus—question, issue, trouble—the text can emerge in a kind of juxtaposed form. That is, the textual exploration may include *both* issue *and* resolution—generally one explicitly and the other implicitly. It is the preacher's holistic moment of insight, grasping both issue and resolution together (sometimes at an intuitive level of thought), that produces the euphoric epistemological experience to begin with. *Perceived connection* between issue and resolution is the key to that uncertain certainty. The connection prompts the excitement—and alerts the preacher that something is happening—even if not yet quite nameable.

On the other hand, when the biblical question is put in the form of resolutional language ("What is the message of the text?"), it is likely that no excitement of juxtaposition will occur. When the biblical question is put in focus language ("What is the issue here?") chances increase that an explicit question may get linked with an implicit answer or an explicit answer may get linked with an implicit question. And one increases greatly the chance of being able to say, "I think I've got something!" Otherwise put, *how* one asks biblical questions is instrumental in determining whether the preacher or the text is doing the driving.

No doubt you have already noticed that I did not suggest the formulation of a theme sentence—which is the more usual advice. Why not? The reasons are multiple—and involve further preparation traps that need to be avoided. First, however, we need to note the important goal that the theme sentence attempts to accomplish. I see its primary goal as providing precision of homiletical purpose. Indeed, through the years I have heard altogether too many sermons (some of them mine) that have wandered all over God's creation looking for a place to land. Sometimes the preacher's desperation (and the listeners' as well) can be resolved only by a lengthy closing summary prayer.

Homiletical precision is, of course, required. The question is how to achieve it. Although often recommended as the answer, theme sentences also provide potential problems. First, a theme sentence tends to propositionalize the sermon. Often the sermonic goal becomes narrowed to an educational aim—to inform, to clarify, to apply, to amplify. And then we measure our success in terms of having "gotten it across"—a very telling phrase. It is too often the case that in the preparation process, the sooner we settle on a theme, the quicker and more likely the sermon can settle on becoming a report.

Second, except in unusual hands, theme sentences often have the effect of turning off the mind. The simple reason is that it names next Sunday's event in terms of *resolution*. Lost is the *torque of juxtaposition*. My experience is that most students who operate with the use of a theme sentence operate deductively as soon as the theme sentence is named. The probing sense of inquiry is lessened, the focus narrowed to "thoughtful and careful" articulation of an informational message.

Now, obviously, this does not always happen. There are those who can utilize the technique with fine effect—but generally they are those whose thinking is wonderfully weird, who are able to see resolution and yet still keep the doors of the mind open. For many, the comfort of resolution is too good to set aside for further engagement of an issue.

Those who suggest a thematic statement often place it exactly between biblical work and sermon formation. The unintended result is to divide the work, with the whole process unwittingly imagined as an hourglass on its side—with biblical work narrowing toward the thematic sentence, which then opens into sermon formation. I believe this to be an unnecessary—even counterproductive—division of labor. The context of sermon formation is often the propitious time for exegetical labor, just as the shape of a biblical text itself can be instructive toward the eventual form of the sermon. How often it has been true for me that if I had to write a theme statement, I would be unable to name it until almost the end of the preparation process! Moreover, once a theme sentence is produced, the preacher tends to move into the driver's seat and take charge.

In short, we need to maximize our capacity to keep open throughout the preparation process. The theme sentence often seems to discourage that openness.

Given the need for precision of purpose, and the problems argued here, I propose the *focus* sentence rather than the *theme* sentence. I have found it remarkable how once the issue is named with some precision, further major questions of the sermon-to-be fall into place. Once the issue is named crisply, the sermonic aim gains focus. My choice in asking for the naming of a sermonic aim is quite deliberate. To perceive the matter as looking for a sermonic message, for example, is too restrictive. What I need to know is, What do I hope will *happen* as a result of this sermon—not, What is its theme, message, or point?

With clarity about focus or issue, the aim becomes more easily nameable. Likewise, when at one end of the anticipated sermonic process I can state the issue and, at the other, the sermonic aim, I am in a better position to figure out what is needed to traverse the gap between. In other words, I am ready to discover the fundamental *turn* of the sermon. Otherwise put: How can the gospel effect the transformation of issue to resolution?

Sometimes the preparation process does not move from focus to aim to turn—sometimes it moves from focus to *turn* to aim (which more nearly resembles the completed sermon). That is, once the issue is named, biblical and other theological work may reveal "from out of the blue" what the sermon really ought to accomplish. In whatever order the second and third major moments in sermon preparation occur, focus almost always comes first.

So it is that the major difference between my advice and others' in imagining preliminary sermon preparation work is clear. I attempt to achieve the important goal of precision by how I ask the sermonic *question* rather than by how I state the sermonic *answer*.

We began our consideration of sermon preparation by means of an image of the "homiletical rabbit"—asking just how we can intentionally and inadvertently allow the rabbit to catch us. Changing the metaphor, the question became one of how to stay out of the driver's seat while preparing our sermon. The issue has to do with authority and control. Advising anyone to "stay open" may seem like the advice to "be spontaneous now." Although it is difficult for a person to decide to stay open in preparation work, there are behaviors that, by their nature, lead us toward openness, and others that will lead us toward control.

My proposal is to move toward a focus statement rather than a theme sentence in order to maximize the chances of remaining open to hear the text. To be sure, survival in sermon preparation is difficult for all. The bottom line finally is not the question of whether we survived. The question is, Did the rabbit survive?

Eugene L. Lowry is William K. McElvaney Professor of Preaching, Emeritus, at Saint Paul School of Theology, Kansas City, Missouri.

5

EVENING PRAYER

The Unexpected Word

Numbers 11:1–17, 24–30
Jane Sigloh

THE ISRAELITES were ready to leave Sinai. They had packed the menorah and the libation bowls, the cups and the jars. They had folded the linen curtains from around the tabernacle. Every tribe was in its proper place. Some on the front row. Some on the back.

And they knew all the rules. Backwards and forwards. If someone is unclean, he stays outside the camp. If a man wrongs his neighbor, he brings a ram of atonement to the altar. If a woman is unfaithful, she drinks the water of bitterness. If a man is unfaithful . . . well, not to worry.

They knew the rules, so at the break of dawn, the trumpets sounded. Bright and clear as reveille. The Levites lifted the ark of the covenant up onto their shoulders. And with a song in their hearts, Israel began to march away from Sinai toward the land of promise.

It was a good day, that first one. And so was the next. But on the third day . . . on the third day the people began to murmur. "Manna. Manna. Manna. Every night it's manna for supper again. Remember the fish we used to eat in Egypt? And the cucumbers and melons and leeks? Now all we get is this flaky stuff. Like . . . BORING!"

Well, Moses heard all this murmuring. And it made him weary. "Why did you give me such a congregation, Lord? Did I conceive them? Did I bring them forth that you should say to me, 'Carry them in your bosom as a woman carries a nursing child?' Here we are in the middle of this desert—the ground is cracking under our feet. And they complain about the bread of heaven—manna that falls like sweet rain—right into our hands. Lord, I'm not quitting, but this is going to be a long trip."

Well, God was very responsive to his servant Moses. "Tell you what I'm gonna do. You bring me seventy elders out to the camp, and I will put some of my spirit upon them so that you won't have to bear the burden of these people all alone." And it was so. The elders went forth and they called the camp meeting the Preaching Excellence Conference.

And the seventy elders began to preach. Did they ever preach! With power and great wisdom. They were faithful to the texts. Without being bound by the intricacies of higher criticism. Or the platitudes of biblicism. They were well versed in moves and structures. Practiced in the art and liturgy of the embodied Word. They built homiletical plots and designed strategies of integration. And their language was precise—but not too fancy—none of those five-syllable words. They preached long after evening had settled on the camp, and no one complained. Indeed they liked it—kept shouting, "Bring it home, brother!"

But that Spirit? The Spirit that settled on the elders? Well, it has a will of its own. It's not restricted by rubrics or rules or proper places around a tabernacle. It spills over like the wind. And settles wherever. Even on strangers who haven't yet learned about strategies of integration. And this time it settled on a man named Eldad and a woman named Medad.

Now Eldad and Medad weren't like the elders. They were young. Really young. Still in their fifties! Thirties even! And suddenly they found themselves in the pulpit. In front of them were pieces of paper, penciled over, corrected, rewritten. And they protested, "I do not know my way with God's word! What am I doing here? Spirit, go away and come again another day!"

But slowly they turned their ear to their heart and listened. Listened until they found their own preaching voices. And then they remembered. Stories of their mothers and fathers. Stories of how Sarah and Abraham were called out of barrenness and futility to a new life in Canaan. And of how difficult it was for them to believe in the promise. "A child in my old age? In your dreams!"

They told how the face of God often seemed to be set against them. "Take your son, your only son, Isaac, and go to the land of Moriah." And about life in Egypt, when their masters refused to give them straw for the bricks—"Gather your own straw!" And how their family labored all day under the whip and were bound in chains at night—far from the home they loved. And how they whispered, "Do, Lord, do remember me."

And then, then they told about the high walls of water, sweeping up to the sky, so that only a few puddles were left on the floor of the sea. And how their parents were carried across on eagles' wings.

It was wonderful. And something extraordinary happened at that camp meeting. The people out there in the congregation began to hear for the first time their own crushed voices brought to public speech. Not petulant voices complaining about food, but beneath the petulance to the deeper voices of grief denied, of anger stifled, loneliness hushed, injustice dismissed, dignity destroyed. The stories of their ancestors enfolded them, gathered them into conversation until they said, "I've been there. I know what they were going through."

And in spite of the grief and anger and injustice—or maybe it was because of the grief and anger and injustice—they forgot their murmuring and began to sing in gratitude. For the walls of water, for the eagles' wings, the precious manna. With great gladness they began to sing: "When from bondage we are summoned, out of darkness into light." And they broke bread together. And celebrated the Great Nevertheless with a doxology that danced like sunlight on dark pools.

Over the next few years Eldad and Medad nurtured the Spirit that had landed on their heads. They studied how to shape, refine, edit, integrate, illustrate. *Shorten!* They took notes, asked the elders to share their expertise. How do you do it without a script? They practiced—climbed the steps and looked out at the empty church. "Prompt me, Lord, prompt me. For I do not know how to meet these people where they are."

And the more they studied, the more they began to see something fresh in the Word. Something that startled them into a new gladness. A single line, a phrase. And they knew that there was still more to be said. There was yet another generation. And they could cross the Jordan River if they wanted. It was right up there just a ways, waiting for them. Even now their children were playing by the banks, throwing rocks in the water. And on the other side . . . the other side?

Eldad and Medad began to prophesy again. They turned to the elders and said, "It's not over! Yours is not the last word! They say a Messiah will be born over there. He will call us home, put his arms around our shoulders and forgive us before we even ask. Forgive us for all those rules we break, day in and day out. Forgive us for our unclean spirit. He will be the cornerstone of a new tabernacle—a whole wonderful tabernacle that stretches out to every corner of the earth.

"Then he will die, and in that death he will gather all the pain of the world into his flesh and bones. All of it—even that of our ancestors who were slaves in Egypt. Then he will roll away the stone from his grave and walk into the light. And when that day comes, we will no longer be strangers wandering across the dessert. We will be members of his household—living right there with him—sharing a meal of gladness. So great is his love."

And hearing these words of prophesy—hearing them flung out across the pews and classrooms, and feeling the burdens of their vocation fall like mantles from their shoulders . . . the elders smiled.

Jane Sigloh is rector emeritus of Emmanuel Episcopal Church in Staunton, Virginia, and a conference leader in preaching and spirituality.

A New Call?

Exodus 3:1–12
William Hethcock

DO YOU recall how Moses got into the land of Midian in the first place? Well, even though Moses had been brought up among the Egyptian royals, he seems to have been aware that he was a Hebrew. One day, after he had grown up to be a man, he went out among these remarkable building projects that Pharaoh was having erected. Moses discovered something very disturbing: that the Hebrew people were experiencing a harsh and burdensome slavery as they went about doing the difficult and painful tasks that made all this building possible. When he looked, "[H]e saw an Egyptian beating a Hebrew, one of his kinsfolk." And so Moses looked all around to see who was watching, and, seeing no one, he killed the Egyptian and buried his body in the sand.

The next day, as he walked among the slaves, he came upon two Hebrews fighting. He asked them why, since they were kinsmen, they would strike one another, and one of them recalled to him what he had done the day before to the Egyptian, saying, "Do you mean to kill me as you killed the Egyptian?"

Moses was suddenly filled with fear, because someone had obviously seen him do murder. It was then that he fled to Midian. Through kindness, he met a benevolent family. He came to marry Zipporah, the daughter of Jethro, his host, and they started a family.

And so it is years later, when Moses is in the employ of his father-in-law as a shepherd, tending the old man's sheep in the land of Midian. Wandering one day, Moses and his flock come upon a striking phenomenon. Over to the side of his way, a bush is burning, and an angel appears in the fire. As he watches, Moses observes a remarkable thing—this bush on fire never seems to burn up. "This is worth investigating," he says to himself, and so he goes over to see what this strange thing may mean.

Before he can reach the fire, Moses hears the voice of God calling his name. "Moses! Moses!" God says, and Moses answers, "Here I am." God tells Moses to remove his sandals, because he is actually on holy ground. And God forbids Moses to come any closer.

This is when Moses, the shepherd, on the lam from the law of the Egyptians, likely bored out of his mind with watching sheep, experiences the life-changing moment that makes things different forever. Not only for him, but for all the people of the Hebrews. The voice is identified: It is the voice of God. "I am the God of your father, Moses, the God of Abraham and Isaac and Jacob." And Moses hides his face, for he is afraid to look at God.

And this is where God calls Moses to a new vocation, one that is beyond Moses' imagination and, he thinks, also beyond what he is able to do. God's voice from the bush recounts to Moses the suffering of the Hebrew people under the cruel power of the Pharaoh, and God reminds Moses of God's ancient promise to lead these chosen people to a land of plenty. And the clincher to God's sermonette is what comes to Moses as a proposition beyond imagination and possibility: "And so, Moses, I will send you to Pharaoh to bring my people, the Israelites, out of Egypt."

Suddenly, for Moses, tending sheep isn't so bad after all. Somehow it seems safer to work in the employ of his father-in-law Jethro, Zipporah's dad, than for Almighty God. And there follows his fruitless plea to be spared such a vocation. With his face hidden, his feet bare, his sheep straying away, and the bush still burning, it occurs to Moses to say, "Who am I that I should go to Pharaoh, and bring the Israelites out of Egypt?" And it appears to us, as we consider this scene, that Moses does indeed have strong points in his favor!

Why in the world would a sensible God take this wandering shepherd, a murderer and a fugitive, someone hiding out among people not his own, distanced from God's land and God's chosen, and make this person the one to free the people of God from Pharaoh's yoke, and lead all of God's people to the promised land? Not even Charlton Heston and Cecil B. DeMille could bring off this miracle without special effects. What is God thinking?

God, this Moses is a nobody, a wimpish pseudo-Egyptian prince, who has been a luxury-loving phony all his life. He can't do it, and your choice is lousy, and we're telling you so, even if you are God!

As usual, God knows something we have forgotten. Look back there at what it was that broke through Moses' pampered consciousness and made him take heed. What we learned a few moments ago is that Moses, from his youth, was actually embracing this holy purpose of his life. Moses, from his young years, had a history as a divine liberator, a person generous in his concern for those who were suffering and downtrodden. Moses cared greatly about the well-being of his kinspeople, God's people; and he was already, at a young age, dedicated to the course of freeing his kin from bondage.

God speaks to Moses where he lives. God says, "I have observed the misery of my people who are in Egypt; I have heard their cry on account of their taskmasters. Indeed, I know their sufferings, and I have come down to deliver them from the Egyptians, and to bring them up out of that land to a good and broad land, a land flowing with milk and honey, to the country [I have promised them]." What seems to be going on with God is that God has been watching Moses; and, as nondescript, directionless, unexciting, and unlikely as Moses is, God sees something there that God can use. Moses loves his people, and he is willing to fight for them. And so, when Moses tries to beg off, God knows what God is doing. God doesn't even listen to Moses. God just keeps on being on fire and telling Moses what he must do until Moses gives in and says, "Well, if you say so, okay."

Look at what is happening. Does Moses have a new calling? Does Moses have a new vocation? Does Moses have a new job? Well, in a sense, yes. But also, in a sense, no, he doesn't. God in God's wisdom is picking Moses out to get him to do what he is already of a mind to do. God is choosing Moses to free the people of Israel with the same passion God saw in Moses when he struck the Egyptian taskmaster. God's divine resolve, to free God's own people, is a lot like Moses' human proclivity, and so that human proclivity, combined with God's resolve, becomes this rather insignificant man's divine calling and vocation.

What if it were to be the case that God actually does not call us to tasks that require of us a complete makeover from scratch? What if, instead, the nature of God's call to humankind is a call in which God will take who we are and what we are, and direct those things we already have to purposes that are God's—purposes beyond our imagination? This tells us something about a call from God. The call that comes to us from God is not a call to become something we are not, but it is a call to use what we already have and who we already are.

Such a truth as that, I think, puts a new light on our struggles. Some of us, in our efforts to respond to God's call, are trying to do an impossible thing. We are trying to become someone we are not. And all the time, what God is saying is that what God wants of us is for us to use the gifts we already have.

What do you suppose is involved in the making of a lawyer, a surgeon, a plumber, or a grocer? Theoretically and, quite possibly, realistically, everyone in this room could be any one of those four persons. I think I could be. It would bore me to death, but I could read for a law degree. And I might get sick to my stomach a few times, but I could learn to be a surgeon. And though vegetables are okay, but not my real concern, I could learn to hose down the asparagus and the beans so that you would buy them even if you don't like them. And I could be a plumber whose straight flush would beat your full house.

But what if my heart really was not in it, and what if I really found no delight or purpose in it? Eventually, my clients and my customers would know, and I would be miserable, as many people are in their work. There is nothing in me, latent or active, that points me toward any of those vocations.

A wonderful student at our school one time, actually, a refugee from a strife-torn African state, came to prepare for ordination to the priesthood. Her sermons were terrible. We kept asking her why she spoke in such a formal and stilted manner. Then one day she gave us a beautiful sermon in which were woven her own story, and her feelings of love and grace for a gospel that had seen her through a good deal of violence and tragedy. And, of course, as you can imagine, her sermon moved all of us. She explained that she had been imitating the formalized sermon style of preachers in her homeland. While it certainly works there, it won't work here. She discovered that; and her sermons became so much a part of her that they were rich with power and strength as well as grace. And they still are today.

One student, whose sermons had been a little on the tedious side, came into chapel one day and preached a really fine sermon. Being the teacher that I am, I asked him what he had done in preparation for that sermon that was different—since, obviously, it was a good strategy, and he should use it again. He said to me, "Well, I finally stopped doing what you told me to do, and did what I thought I should have been doing all alone." From that, both of us learned.

A call, a vocation, it turns out, is much more about a longing to do what needs to be done than a skill at doing it. A call is much more about a passion for what the call is, than mere training to learn how to do it. A call is much more about spending the parts of one's self that are needed by the enterprise at hand, than it is becoming somebody we are not. A call is much more about faithfulness to God than merely believing in God. Learning the skills is no substitute for being the person. A vocation, it comes to be, is a call to be who we already are, and letting our talents be discovered, developed, honed, beautified, and given. Somehow it seems to me that what God wants is round pegs in round holes, and square pegs in square holes.

Let me try this with you. You see what you think. What is the nature of God's call to you? Is it a call to be someone very different from who you were when all this started? Maybe God isn't really calling you to be a different person. What if, instead, God is reaching inside you to find those things God needs and to call you to make use of them in God's name?

I think that's the idea we get here from Scripture. When you look at what Moses' real passion is—caring for his people, the people of God, and defending them—then God's call isn't so strange. Actually, God comes to be smarter than we thought. God seeks out the person who is already on the way and says, "You are the one I want for what I plan to do."

And so, when Moses says he's a nobody with improper credentials, God says, "So what?" When Moses says he's no public speaker, God ignores him. When Moses says, "But I don't even know your name," God says, "Neither does anyone else."

"But I'll tell you this, Moses," says God. "I will be with you through all this." And, as it came about, God was with him, and that was all Moses needed.

William Hethcock is professor of homiletics, emeritus, at the School of Theology in the University of the South, Sewanee, Tennessee.

THE FEAST OF BONIFACE

The Dream of God

Luke 24:44–53
James P. Adams

THE POET Robert Frost had some advice for preachers. "A good sermon," he said, "should have an interesting beginning and an interesting ending; and the two should be as close together as possible." Today we are given a small Gospel; but one that points to a big dream.

I think of a girl from my class in high school. Her name was Eve, Eve Morrisey. Eve was a petite girl, maybe five feet tall and very thin. Her eyes were bright and blue as the bluest sky you've ever seen. Her hair color was, most of the time, sandy brown, but subject to change without notice. She sported a high-style haircut, the kind you often see in photographs on the walls of the hair salon but almost never on a real person. Though we shared a friend or two in common, Eve Morrisey was not a close friend of mine. So, why do I think of her now?

I remember Eve Morrisey because she was a great performer, a talented actress, and a gifted singer. She had one of those rare, soul-stirring soprano voices that can turn even the stiffest Episcopalian into a bowl full of jelly. Eve possessed a certain inner fire that radiated from her when she stepped onto the stage. Eve was also a dreamer. She barely made it through high school, doing just enough work to get by, ignoring what the teachers said, while visions of plum parts on Broadway danced in her head. Those of us who knew her believed that one day Eve's dream, her dream of singing and dancing on Broadway would come true.

In the lesson from the Gospel this morning, Jesus begins to explain God's plan for drawing the world to himself. After all that he has done, after the agony of the cross and the glory of the resurrection, Jesus has finished the piece of the mission that he took on flesh to accomplish. It is time for him to go. He looks at his gathered followers—there are fewer than twenty people there. They stare at him in awe: waiting . . . waiting to hear how he plans to share the power of his risen life with the rest of the world. And then, when his disciples can stand it no more, Jesus speaks: "Tag," he says, "you're it!"

"I am sending upon you what my Father promised," Jesus says, "so stay here in the city until you have been clothed with power from on high." And then he leaves them.

"Tag, we're it!" The God who spoke the world into being and appeared to Moses in a burning bush took on flesh and bone like ours to usher in his dream of the Kingdom of God; and now he leaves his mission of mercy in our hands. God knows we can't do it alone. We don't have what it takes. Jesus knows we are not ready for prime time; and so, he says, we are to wait for the outpouring of the Holy Spirit. The promise of the Holy Spirit is a promise of abundant life—love and joy overflowing from God.

If we are to accept such an extravagant gift, how will we prepare a place in our hearts? This is the holy work to which Jesus calls us today. If the truth is told, we have compromised too much in our lives when it comes to joy and love. Our lives have a certain contented "curb appeal" but, if the truth is told, in the undercrofts of our hearts, we all mourn secret losses, and we all nurse wounds that are known to us alone. Maybe preparing a place for the coming of the Holy Spirit means paying attention to the longings of our hearts in a new way. Maybe we have kept God up here in our heads and away from our hearts because we are afraid God might change us. Well, God has work to do in our hearts. If you have ever been in love with another person, then you have had a taste of the transforming power of God's love.

When we are truly in love, our beloved reveals in us a person who is wiser, more beautiful, smarter, funnier, sexier, and more interesting than we ever thought we could be. I think of the film *As Good As It Gets*. Jack Nicholson tells the woman he loves, "You make me want to be a better man." God's upward call. This is what Jesus gives us today. Not a set of rules or obligations, but a love that changes us, that softens our hearts for the coming of the Holy Spirit. Jesus has chosen us to carry on his mission. We are not ready to take on that mission, but his love can make us ready. He makes me want to be a better man.

The American novelist Wallace Stegner was given a mighty taste of God's transforming love in his mother. He wrote an open letter to her, fifty-five years after she died, as he was approaching his own eightieth birthday. He calls it "A Letter Much Too Late." Stegner writes (in part):

> Mother, listen. Fifty-five years ago, sitting up with you after midnight while the nurse rested, I watched you take your last breath. A few minutes before you died, you raised your head and said, "Which . . . way?" I understood that you were at a dark, unmarked crossing. Then a minute later you said, "You're a good . . . boy . . . Wallace," and you died. My name was the last word you spoke; your faith in me, and love for me, were your last thoughts. I could bear them no better than I could bear your death, and I went blindly out into the November darkness and walked for hours with my mind clenched like a fist. I knew how far from true your last words were. There had been plenty of times when I had not been a good boy or a thought-ful one. I knew that it was love speaking, not you, that you had already gone, that your love lasted longer than you yourself did.[1]

Stegner goes on to say that his mother's love for him was a commission for the rest of his life. He says that he never got over trying to be the man his mother thought he was. Her love enlarged and deepened him. She made him want to be a better man.

The world doesn't need more perfect people or people pretending to be perfect. The world needs people who have been touched by God's transforming love, and who are willing to talk about it.

God's dream. Do you dare believe that God has a dream for your life? God dreams of you, awakening to see his hand in what seems most ordi-nary. Consider the beating of your heart, the movement of your fingers, your eyes and your voice. Think of the mystery of resting your head on a pillow, falling fast asleep, and of waking again. God dreams that today you will see everything in your life as a gift and a holy mystery.

A priest is working on his Sunday sermon when he is interrupted by his child insisting that she needs his help on the toilet. He finally goes to help, but he is unhappy with this interruption of his "holy" work. It is only later, when he carries his little girl to her room and tucks her into bed, that he is awakened to the holiness of her need, the sacredness of her trust, and the meaning of his service.

Imagine seeing everything we do as an act of praise and thanksgiving. Raising a garden, raising money, and raising a family can be worship. In

God's dream, making dinner, making beds, and making love are transforming liturgies of praise and thanksgiving. In God's dream, mending a broken relationship and mending an old coat are holy work. When our life and worship become one piece, we are enlarged and deepened, and God's dream for us begins to come true.

I wish I could tell you that Eve Morrisey made it big on Broadway. I cannot, because I have no idea whatever became of her. Last I knew (fifteen years ago) she was dating a boy from Cleveland. Maybe she is married to him now, and maybe she leads the drama club for her own children in the middle school there. Maybe something in college spoke to her, and maybe she practices law or medicine in Boston now. Or maybe she waits tables at a diner in Hartford, and sings sad songs in the shower at night. Who knows? God knows. And yet, in my mind, she is still eighteen; and when my wife and I saw the musical *Cats* on Broadway, I must tell you that I looked for Eve among all those radiant, dreamy-eyed cats.

God's dream for Eve, and for you and me, is much bigger than a leading role on Broadway, or in business, or in the church. God delights in the things that bring us joy; but our dreams are always too small. Today, God's dream takes center stage; and if we give him half a chance, God will do in us infinitely more than we can ask or imagine.

James P. Adams is rector of St. Alban's Church,
Cape Elizabeth, Maine.

---

1. Wallace Stegner, *Where the Bluebird Sings to the Lemonade Springs*, New York: Penguin-Putnam, Inc., 1992, p. 22–23.

EVENING PRAYER

What's in a Name?

Joshua 1:1–9
Linda L. Clader

I HAVE to admit I've always felt a little jealous of people who were named after somebody. I always imagine that knowing you were named after a great-grandparent or another ancestor would make you feel more tied into the past, the family tradition, maybe a family set of values.

And then there are the heroes, and the saints. Some of you have met my husband, Nick, who is sort of lurking around the edges of this conference. He's really Robert Nicholas, but he's always gone by "Nick." And there's no doubt that he feels connected with that saint of the same name. I asked him if I could talk with you about this, and I told him I was going to say he identified with Saint Nick. He said, "No, I don't!"

But *I* know better! You should see our house in December. *Nobody* needs as many St. Nicholases as we have, set up sometimes two and three deep on tables and shelves. It starts on the Feast of St. Nicholas, December sixth, and continues on from there. "But that's just the season!" I hear you say. "Lots of people go overboard during the holidays." Right. True. But does everybody have a three-foot-high carved wooden bishop on their dining room wall—all year round?

St. Nicholas—patron saint of sailors, children, and prostitutes. Is it only coincidence that my Nick, who bears the saint's name, has embraced a ministry to those whom society tries to push to the fringes— prisoners, the poor, the mentally ill? Is it only a coincidence? I wonder.

So the twelve or thirteen years that I've been watching this St. Nicholas phenomenon have led me to ask a similar question about Joshua. Well, not really about Joshua, the son of Nun. The question I'm asking is about that other Joshua, Joshua of Nazareth, Joshua ben Joseph, the man the Greeks called Iesous, the man we call the Christ. Joshua of Nazareth, whose name was given to him by God and announced by an angel—I wonder how *that* young Joshua related to Joshua, son of Nun, the hero of his people's story, the hero whose name he bore?

When Joshua of Nazareth heard the story about Moses laying his hands on Joshua, son of Nun, did he imagine himself kneeling before Moses, too? When he heard about the Lord appearing to Moses and Joshua in the pillar of cloud, commissioning Joshua to lead the Israelites into the promised land—did he *dream* about how he might lead those same children? What about that story of Eldad and Medad we heard the day before yesterday—the story where Joshua objected to Moses that people who hadn't been *ordained* were prophesying? Did he listen when Moses celebrated the spirit of the Lord resting on *unplanned* people? Did he take that concept in?

And what about when he heard that God commanded Joshua, son of Nun, to be strong and very courageous, and to be careful to act in accordance with *all the Law of Moses*? And when he heard God promise to be with Joshua "wherever he went"? Did Joshua of Nazareth hear that command—and that promise—and imagine it applying especially to *him*? And when Joshua of Nazareth embarked on his adult ministry of teaching and healing, and his prophetic acts—was Joshua, son of Nun, alive and active in his imagination?

Looking back from here—post-Hiroshima, and post-Vietnam, post-Korea, post–Gulf War, and if I look back through the hazy justice of modern Israel's treatment of her neighbors—looking back from here, I have a few difficulties with the heroic figure of Joshua, son of Nun. I have trouble with his destruction of the city of Ai, killing twelve thousand men, women, and children. I have trouble with Joshua hamstringing horses, and hanging the five kings from trees. Could Jesus—Joshua of Nazareth—could he have identified with *that?* Could he really have identified with a bloody war hero?

Maybe, like us, Jesus was able to hear the heroic stories of his ancestors, and use them as metaphors, allegories, or parables. Maybe he could listen to the bloody stories of Joshua, son of Nun, conquering the promised land—maybe he could hear all that, and translate it into a celebration of the glorious coming of the Reign of God. Maybe the blood and guts of the old stories were a way of underlining how important it all was—that through the story shone the great goodness of God's gift of the Law to God's people: the Law that guaranteed justice over revenge, the Law that commanded compassion to foreigners and mercy to the poor, the Law that understood how the earth belonged to God, and how the people who lived there were simply stewards.

Maybe when Jesus heard the stories of Joshua, son of Nun, he could reach back in his imagination to a time when the Law of Moses was fresh, to a time when it hadn't been turned into an excuse for pushing the weak to society's margins—a time when the Law *itself* was a promise of freedom to captives, sight to the blind, and good news to the poor.

"Only be strong and very courageous," said the Lord. "Being careful to act in accordance with *all the Law* that my servant Moses commanded you . . . that you may be successful wherever you go."

Joshua, who brought a law of equality into a land of tyranny—Joshua, who was faithful to the Lord when others faltered and ran—Joshua, man of fierce spirit and courage and hope—Joshua, who learned from Moses that the Lord could send the spirit of prophecy onto people whose credentials hadn't quite been confirmed—maybe those were the things Joshua of Nazareth thought about when he heard the old stories about the hero whose name now rested on him.

Maybe, just maybe, the shadow of that ancient Joshua, son of Nun, hovered over the later Joshua's life, forming his imagination, challenging him as he defined his ministry and his message, and strengthening him with the promise of Yahweh: "Be strong and courageous; do not be frightened or dismayed, for the LORD your God is with you wherever you go."

Do you think that Joshua of Nazareth remembered that promise? Do you think any of that beat in his heart? Do you think that promise encouraged him to imagine the Reign of God into the here and now? Do you think it emboldened him to *walk* that Reign of God *in the flesh?* I bet it did.

I was reading a homiletics text the other day that presented preachers with a system of exegesis. Actually, any number of homiletics books on the market today echo with this same advice: "As you study the pericope, look for Law and Gospel, Law and Gospel." First, explore how we are convicted by the Law, then reveal how we're freed by the Good News of Jesus Christ.

I'm not going to dispute the usefulness of naming our failings and our sins, and our ability to erect barriers against grace. And this approach does offer a system that can result in a neat balance, or "homiletical plot."

But beware of a false dichotomy here. It's all too easy to fall into a simplistic equation—a distortion of what St. Paul was really talking about. "*Law equals repression and slavery; Gospel* equals *redemption and freedom.* Law—Bad! Gospel—Good!"

From there it's another easy step to "Hebrew Bible—Old; New Testament—New, Hebrew Bible—Incomplete; New Testament—Complete. Hebrew Bible—Wrong; New Testament—Right." And from there it's easy to slide further to a truly destructive claim that we have been set free from all the error of the old, and the non-Christian, and the "Other."

Far be it from us preachers to begin sliding down that slippery slope—because as we pick up momentum, we find ourselves offering Scriptural refuge—homiletical refuge—to those of us who want an excuse to dismiss what is old, to condemn the non-Christian, to push to the margins those who are different from ourselves.

But we preachers have been baptized into the life and the death and the *name* of Joshua of Nazareth, and so we simply have no excuse to fall into anything like that! Baptized into Joshua the Christ, we are baptized into the *courage* of the warrior, and into the *hope* of the prophet. Baptized into Joshua the Christ, we recognize that the Spirit of God often rests on people who surprise us, and we come to expect that through those strange vehicles God can accomplish things that are illogical, unlikely, even impossible.

Baptized into Joshua the Christ, we are heirs of the ancient, revolutionary justice of God, the Law that offers freedom and hope. Baptized into his Body, bearing his Name, we are taken into the ancient story, into the tradition that formed him—with its challenge, and its promise, and its call to invite everyone we meet to enter with us into that Promised

Land of God's Reign: "Be strong and courageous; do not be frightened or dismayed, for the LORD your God is with you wherever you go."

Linda L. Clader is associate professor of homiletics at the Church Divinity School of the Pacific in Berkeley, California.

TUESDAY IN THE SEVENTH WEEK OF EASTER

"Do Not Shrink from Doing Anything Helpful"

Acts 20:17–27
William J. Eakins

I SUSPECT that the reason each of us is here in this chapel this morning is that there has been a Miss Pfost in our lives. There has been someone who spoke to us of God's loving purpose and the world's sore need in such a way that we said, "Here am I, send me." Miss Pfost was my first preaching parent. She never saw the inside of a pulpit, for she was not a preacher, but a teacher. Yet I know it is to Miss Pfost that I owe my own first stirring of a sense of mission.

Miss Pfost taught my kindergarten class at the Gateway Christian School in Hackensack, New Jersey; and I loved her with all the devotion of my five-year-old heart. So one day, when Miss Pfost told us about the work of the Ramaby Mukti Mission in India, I was all ears. The mission was engaged in the rescue of little girls, unwanted by their parents, who were left in the jungle at night to be eaten by tigers. The Ramaby Mukti missionaries would listen for the little girls' cries, run out into the dark jungle, pick them up before the tigers got to them, and take the girls back to the mission. There the girls would be given a home where they would be safe and loved—and even more important, be told the Good News about Jesus and about God's love for them.

I was deeply touched by this missionary story, and wanted to do something to keep saving those little girls from the tigers, so they could grow up learning about Jesus. I went home that day and emptied my piggy bank to give all that I had for the work of the Ramaby Mukti Mission. It was the first step on the journey that led me to ordination as deacon and priest, and to the past thirty-one years of parish ministry, working to make the Word of God heard.

Who was your Miss Pfost? Who stirred your soul to take up the task of mission, to be the ones called out and sent to the world on God's behalf? I'm sure God sent a Miss Pfost to you, because that is always God's way. The word of God comes to Isaiah, sending him as a prophet, not just to his own people Israel, but to all the nations on earth. And the apostles are given the great commission to "go and make disciples of all nations."

While each of us knows that we have been called to mission, what we also have in common, if we have thought at all seriously about our calling, is the experience of being overwhelmed. Consider, for example, the task of preaching. Most of us find it hard enough to preach in our own pulpits, let alone to all the world. How, in heaven's name, are we, week after week, year after year, going to find something to say to our congregations, and not just "something," but the Word of God that will speak to the urgent needs of the people God loves?

Preaching Excellence Program students, have you known a little terror here this week? Have your knees not knocked a bit, as you have stepped up to your makeshift pulpits? And faculty, how about you? Have your evenings been filled with confidence that your exegesis has been thorough, your construction clever, and your message profound? I imagine that each of us has approached our time in the pulpit with fear and trembling. I know that I have. Preaching is a daunting responsibility, and the prerequisite of any preaching worthy of the name is realizing that it is so.

There is an old story of a Scottish Presbyterian minister who climbed into the pulpit brimming with self-confidence. As the sermon progressed, however, the preacher noticed telltale signs that the sermon was not the hit he thought it was going to be. The minister made his final point, concluded quickly, and made his way down from the pulpit visibly humbled. An old Scotsman observing the scene was heard to remark, "Had the preacher gone into the pulpit the way he came down from the pulpit, he might have come down the way he went up." Humility, the recognition of our own limitations and our dependence upon God to direct our speech, is the foundation of any good sermon.

Preachers can take heart because we are like those disciples to whom Jesus gave the great commission: They worshipped him but some doubted. Isn't that an accurate way of describing us as well? We take up the task of preaching in the first place because we are those who worship. God has touched our hearts, and we have been moved to offer ourselves in God's service. And yet we are also doubters. We are full of questions about ourselves, and about our own worthiness to accomplish our mission. And we have questions about God as well. And we should have! There certainly is plenty of mystery to God's ways.

Jesus picked disciples who had doubts. Doubtfulness is not the enemy, but the ally of good preaching. The double-mindedness that makes us question ourselves, that makes us aware of the daunting nature of our responsibility, keeps us humble and dependent upon God. But double-mindedness also enables us to open the door that connects God's world and ours. Yes, every preacher heralds God's reign of justice and love, but unless preachers address the questions that arise in their hearers' minds and hearts, their proclamation will not be heard. And the best way I know for us preachers to be in touch with the questions of our hearers is to recognize the questions we have ourselves.

It is our joy at this season to proclaim the Good News that is the essence of our faith: Christ is risen! The Lord is risen indeed! Those brave and joyous words, however, are only so much liturgical mumbo jumbo unless we test them against some very real questions. Why should I believe Christ is risen? What evidence is there? What difference does it make? If Christ is risen, why are people killing each other in East Timor and Fiji? Why can't my son be healed of his addiction? Why did my husband leave me? Recognizing and addressing such questions is the task of every preacher. It is not, thank God, that the preacher has to answer all the questions (although many foolhardily try), but it is crucial to name our doubts, because it is in relation to those doubts that faith takes on meaning. Congregations don't expect us preachers to have all the answers, but they do expect us to acknowledge their questions, to ask deeper questions yet, and at the same time to proclaim our faith.

Yes, it was to disciples, who worshipped and doubted, that the risen Christ gave the great commission to go into all the world. And it was to those who worshipped and doubted that Christ also gave the great promise: "I am with you always, to the end of the age." What encouragement there is in those words!

Those first disciples, like us would-be preachers, were scared, confused, anxious, unsure of themselves, and the risen Lord spoke words that put the heart back into them. "I am with you always." Remember that I have chosen you. I love you and believe in you. I'm counting on you to go and preach the gospel everywhere. Go teach the faith. Go make new disciples. Go, and I will be with you.

The promise is clear. Preachers have been given a daunting task, a holy mission. But the same God who has called us to this service has also promised to be with us always, to give us, if we will receive it, the wisdom, the passion, and the strength to speak on God's behalf.

Fifty years ago God raised up a teacher of the faith named Miss Pfost, and God gave her a story to tell about little girls in India who needed to hear the Good News about Jesus. God led a little boy into Miss Pfost's classroom to hear that story from the teacher that he loved. And the Lord was present in that classroom and blessed the words of the teacher so that they took root in the heart of the boy and bore fruit beyond the teacher's imagining. So also will the Lord take your words, offered honestly and prayerfully. So go and preach them. Go and make disciples of all nations.

In his valedictory to Christians at Ephesus, St. Paul summarized his work among them: "I did not shrink from doing anything helpful, proclaiming the message to you and teaching you publicly and from house to house." Those words provide a fitting focus for our work as well.

William J. Eakins is rector of Trinity Church,
Hartford, Connecticut.

"You Did Not Choose Me—I Chose You"

1 Samuel 16:1–13
Janice Robinson

"YOU'VE GOT to be kidding, Jan! I can't do that."

"Give it a moment Judy, let it sink in; think about it; and by all means pray about it," I said.

Having a reputation as someone who doesn't mince words, and being a person who can often sound quite angry, Judy thought I had lost my mind when I approached her about becoming a Stephen Minister. "You did not choose me but I chose you," says Jesus (John 15:16).

While we have no knowledge from the text what David thought about the idea of becoming the next king of Israel, I can't imagine that he jumped for joy. A young boy tending sheep on a hillside, focused on playing his harp! Enjoying the simple pleasures of singing and tending the flock is a whole lot better than thinking about how to move a stiff-necked people from one place to another. I can almost hear him saying, "No thanks, I have some sheep to tend for my father."

His elders would not have been far from his line of thinking, I'm sure. "Who is this kid? He's only Jesse's youngest son. He can't even go to war. Who would follow him? Besides, we have Saul for our king, even if he is a royal pain!"

How, indeed, could God call a child, a tender of sheep, a player of the lyre? Not only is he too young to know anything about leadership, he comes from a family that is not known for its wealth, its status in the community, or its power. As a matter of fact, if anyone looks closely (and being a part of a small, agricultural community, people *would* scan Jesse's family chart), they will see that David's ancestry is suspect, at best.

To begin with, his great-grandparents, Ruth and Boaz, were not of the right stock. Ruth, the Moabite immigrant, married Boaz, whose family tree contained a couple of women who did not enjoy the best reputations: Tamar, almost killed for having been raped; and Rahab, best known as a "woman of the night."

"You did not choose me, I chose you." What kind of God is this who would pick people of such lowly status? Knowing David's story, we may well wonder. Here is this upstart warrior who becomes a fugitive and outlaw. Then a mercenary. Once he has power as king, he molests one of his subjects, then tries to cover it up when he learns that she is pregnant. When commanded to do so by Samuel, David's father presents all of his sons except David. Not many would have made the same choice that God made for Israel's next king.

Jesus, when he calls his disciples, calls men who are not learned. They are fishermen, farmers, tax collectors, and the like. They are crude men with no particular status in the community. They are not sought out for their wisdom. Oh, there are those who would ask them a question about fishing, perhaps the best way to mend a net, or the best fishing spots, or the hour they are most likely to catch fish. But lead others to God?

Jesus himself doesn't present a resume that is any great shakes. Born in a stable, of a woman who became pregnant mysteriously, and who was not married to his father at the time. Not only that, but Jesus is raised in a backwater town called Nazareth. How can this man be the anointed of God to lead Israel? What could God be thinking about? "You did not choose me—I chose you."

How did a small boy from a small town in South Africa ever get to be called to be a bishop in the church? How could a diminutive black man armed only with his faith, a great smile, a gentle spirit, some funny jokes, and a prayer, take on a government—and become a reason that one of the most violent, militaristic governments in the world was toppled? "You did not choose me—I chose you."

While we can't read the mind of God, we can get some clues to our questions by looking at what those who are disciples have in common. They are not necessarily people whom we would have chosen for the tasks they were given. They are not attractive according to the notions of their own day. Each is outside of the power structure. None seem, on the surface, to possess leadership qualities; at least they are not part of groups to which others might look for leadership. They are brought along and nurtured for the posts that they are to fill. The human eye cannot see what they have, at least not at the time that they are called by God. As God tells Samuel, "I look at the human heart and not at what you see." Further, God seems to say, "I don't care what they look like; not do I care about whether others think they are ready to take on the tasks I have set for them. I have need of them."

Jesus infers that those whom God calls need to be reality-based. Jesus doesn't want them to have any illusions about what they are getting themselves into by following him. Jesus tells the "wanna-be" in Matthew, "Foxes have holes, and birds of the air have nests; but the Son of Man has nowhere to lay his head"(Matt. 8:20). It is a warning that if you expect to find security, a safe haven from problems or conflicts, don't come this way. Further, Jesus goes on to detail that if they think they can have any other priority but God's business, "Don't bother."

The initiative belongs to Jesus in calling the disciples, not with their making application. Jesus calls disciples into a world that reverses the world's priorities, and so they must be ready to let go of the ideas they have held as most important.

God seems to require the trusting faith that a young child like David can give. Remember the boat trip the disciples took? The disciples follow Jesus into a boat and as the evening wears on a storm arises. Waves so high, they threaten to swamp the boat. Panic sets in among the disciples. Jesus is sleeping in a corner of the boat. The disciples awaken Jesus, crying, "Lord, save us! We are perishing!" Jesus responds, "Why are you afraid, you of little faith?" Jesus rebukes the winds and the sea and suddenly there is dead calm. "What sort of man is this, that even the winds and the sea obey him?" the disciples say, utterly astonished (Matt. 8:25–27). Matthew would have the church see that God is looking for faith that will remain steady even in the midst of trouble, or perhaps especially in the midst of trouble.

God asks for a child's trust. Children, when they are in trouble, turn to adults, believing they can help. This kind of trust is open and will take risks. It's a kind of trust that will allow a person to journey forth without a well-laid-out road map, but only the promise that they will not be alone.

It would seem that God seeks those who are willing to expand their own horizons, even if they are scared. Those who will not become stuck in the way things have always been. God seems to call those who are at least nominally willing to be made uncomfortable, yes, even troubled. "You did not choose me, I chose you." God initiates, we respond. We would do well to remember that without God's grace we couldn't follow God's call to us.

When I spoke to Judy about becoming a Stephen Minister, I was not claiming any of the clarity that belongs to God, only that I was looking for something that would enable her to become a part of the parish community again. Despite the ways in which Judy could alienate others, she genuinely gave a damn about them; and would always speak the truth to them, even when it was hard. Judy needed to know that she could have her care received, and could bring her clarity to bear when another member of the community was in need of being clear. She trusted me; and I trusted that God knew what God was doing in leading me to ask Judy to consider this ministry.

Sometimes we tend not to look beyond the obvious possibilities, though often God calls us to do so. When do we look among those who are often absent from our tables, the poor, those who speak another language, those who think differently from the way we do, who take different positions on things than we do, for leadership? In our own moments of self-estrangement, we don't think that God would see possibilities in us, either.

Despite the fact that Scriptures tell us of God's unexpected choices, we still tend to focus more on appearances and image, and to confuse them with reality. We still buy the right car, the right clothes, the right makeup; the right cleaning agent through appeal to ideas of what is chic, what is macho, what is successful, what is "in." Our political candidates focus their campaigns more on polishing an image than on the content of the issues. They want to appear "right" to those who see them.

God looks at the heart, at our intentions. We must redirect our attention to look as God does, beyond the exterior. David was attractive in appearance, but his heart was most important. God chooses not because we have the "right stuff," but because God has need of us. God calls David, and then pours out the Spirit upon him, empowering him to do the work God has set for him. He is called to help Israel to see and use her own power again, to unify herself, to focus her worship toward God, and to even risk loss for God.

Appearance alone won't do, but the focus of the heart is what matters. Jesus called *together* a community of those who were *marginalized* by their community. They were the least thought of in terms of having something to offer that others could use. Yet it was this ragtag band that was able to bring healing to those who were sick, lame, blind, mentally disordered. This small group of people went into the entire known world at the time and took the Word of hope, the Word of love, and the Word of courage that all might hear and believe.

Discipleship initiated by God is not based upon our appearance to the world. It is not related to how tall we are, what color we are, what language we speak, whom we know, what our stature is in the community.

Rather, it is based upon the condition of our heart. Disciples need to be reality-based and willing to follow without promised security, and with no permanent place to call our own. Discipleship is a risky vocation. Nothing can have a higher priority in our lives. We must be willing to trust God, believe God's promises, and have a willingness to expand our horizons. Receptivity to new ways of thinking, new ways of doing things, and new ways of being in this world.

God initiates and we respond. Our response must be daily. "Today, whom will I serve? How far am I willing to go?"

"You did not choose me—I chose you."

Janice Robinson is rector of Grace Church,
Silver Spring, Maryland.

A VOTIVE FOR THE PREACHING OF THE GOSPEL

Witnesses

Matthew 10: 5–22
Judith M. McDaniel

THE RUBRIC for our worship this morning indicates that this Eucharist is a Votive for the Preaching of the Gospel. A votive. The word evokes images of heads bowed in prayer before candlelit altars, and the taking of solemn vows for grave causes. A votive mass is a serious transaction. This morning we are being asked to pledge ourselves to a sacred duty, to enter into a commitment that involves risk and self disclosure. But the Gospel appointed does not immediately lend itself to such a consecration. The commission being portrayed in these verses is exclusive, and few among us have any interest in propagating an elitist club. Is this passage "impenetrably complex [or just] morally problematic"[1]?

Commitment, risk, self-disclosure on these terms? What kind of vow is the preacher being asked to take?

The remembrance of this episode is recorded in all three Synoptic Gospels, twice in Luke. Clearly this story was important to early Christians. Moreover, the succession of events that frame the account in all three Synoptics is stunningly parallel. The reader is being given a signal.

Something pivotal has happened with this commissioning, a transaction whose consequences will not be turned back.

Listen again to the preliminary instructions, found only in Matthew. These instructions are quite specific: "Go nowhere among the Gentiles, and enter no town of the Samaritans, but go rather to the lost sheep of the house of Israel." Only the house of Israel! Aren't the Gentiles you and me? And, depending on your point of view, aren't the Samaritans only slightly less than full-fledged members of the house of Israel, worshippers in Samaria? The conversation seems to foreshadow Jesus' later encounter with the Canaanite woman, an encounter—Matthew reports—in which the woman appears to teach Jesus of the worthiness of others to eat the crumbs that fall from their masters' table (Matt. 15:26–27). Not only does Jesus say in both these Matthean pericopes that his mission is exclusively to the lost sheep of the house of Israel; but even among those lost, he directs the missionaries four times to seek out only the worthy.

Why all this prioritizing? What is the significance of this segregation of people into "worthy" and "unworthy" listeners? Some commentators dodge those questions by suggesting that the commissioning of these preachers proceeded in two stages: First, they were to proclaim the Good News to the Jews. Then it only logically follows, they argue, that the Gentiles came second. Others point out that the author of the Gospel according to Matthew was writing something like a manual of instructions for the new Israel, the church. Seeking to demonstrate the church's continuity with the faithful remnant of Israel, Matthew takes every opportunity to indicate that Jesus and all that he did were the fulfillment of Old Testament prophecy. And there are other clues that the body of the faithful is expanding: Not only are the instructions to the missionaries to take no copper coins, χαλκόν as Mark records; nor silver, ἀργύριον as Luke reports; but take no copper, no silver, and no χρυσὸν, gold, says Matthew! The church must be doing pretty well! One has to *have* gold, after all, in order to leave it behind. If, then, the church is the established new Israel, for whom is the preacher's restricted message intended?

To deal with this text as if it were simply a history of the charge to go forth and preach Good News to all nations is to miss the essence of the message. There is a prior transaction to be acknowledged, and the text does not yield that transaction through a simple recital of its language. Textual criticism and the historical-critical method are entirely too limited for dealing with the Bible, for text-critical questions circumscribe the answers we can receive. The questions we ask limit the answers. A preacher approaches the Bible with more respect when he or she reflects on it as a poetic text, a transformative vehicle that makes possible an imaginative reconstruction of reality.

Old Testament scholar Ellen Davis writes of establishing such intimacy with the text that it becomes an "echo chamber," reverberating with memories. By means of the metaphor, Davis reminds us that the original recipients of the biblical message heard ancient resonances that those of us less familiar with biblical language struggle to hear. When Jesus' disciples heard the words "the lost sheep of the house of Israel," they heard echoes of a vulnerable God, speaking through the mouth of Ezekiel: "I myself will search for my sheep, and will seek them out" (Matt. 34:12). They heard resonances of Micah: "I will surely gather all of you, O Jacob, I will gather the survivors of Israel; I will set them together like sheep in a fold, like a flock in its pasture; it will resound with people"(Matt. 2:12).

Listening for poetic echoes enables the preacher to hear that this morning's text is not about a heroic people commissioned to preach. This text is about a heroic God who keeps coming back to pick up the pieces.[2] This passage is about a God who is vulnerable to human unfaithfulness, a God who calls others to that same vulnerability, risk, and self-disclosure. Commissioned for vulnerability, the preacher can ask with fresh insight, "To whom is this proclamation directed? With whom does the missionary endeavor begin?"

Listen to the text again, and hear the echoes: "Behold, I send you out as sheep in the midst of wolves; so be wise as serpents and innocent as doves. Beware of men; for they will deliver you up to councils, and flog you in their synagogues, and you will be dragged before governors and kings for my sake, as a witness against them" [εἰς μαρτύριον αὐτοῖς].

Witness. Witness.

And Joshua said to the people at Shechem, "You are witnesses against your own selves, that you yourselves have chosen for yourself the Lord, to serve him." And they said, "Witnesses" (Josh. 24:22).

To whom is Jesus' proclamation directed, and with whom does the witness begin? With the preacher . . . preaching to him- or herself. If you and I are not preaching to our own lostness, our own alienation, our own need for the nearness of God, we will not be preaching to anyone. We proclaim to our own vulnerability, and only then to the vulnerability of others, our need and willingness to change. We witness as we go, not to what we must do, but to what God has done and is doing and will do to bring about that change and to bring God's Kingdom near. On this day we vow, "We are witnesses against our own selves, that we ourselves

have chosen for ourself the Lord, to serve *him*."
Witnesses.

Judith M. McDaniel is professor of homiletics at Virginia
Theological Seminary, Alexandria, Virginia

---

1. Ellen F. Davis, "Losing a Friend: The Loss of the Old Testament to the Church," paper presented to the North American Academy of Homiletics, Toronto, 1998.

2. Stanley Hauerwas and William H. Willimon, *Resident Aliens* (Nashville: Abingdon Press, 1989), p. 57.

EVENING PRAYER

The Truth in Love

Ephesians 4:1–16
Charles Rice

THIS IS a summer of church conventions. The Southern Baptists' deliberations have led them to send women back to the kitchen, and the United Methodists have heard the Bible telling homosexual Christians to stifle themselves and stay in the closet. Soon the Presbyterians will have their turn, and we'll take ours at General Convention in Denver.

We hope, at least, to keep on talking about the things that vex church and society; and perhaps even break through to what the Ephesian writer envisions, that "speaking the truth in love, we [might] grow up in every way into him who is the head, into Christ."

Asia Minor, where this pastoral letter probably circulated—and from whose rich capital city it takes its name—was at the commercial and cultural crossroads of the ancient world. Ephesus, the only city in the world built entirely of marble, and the surrounding region prospered from the trade that moved back and forth between Europe and Asia. No doubt the fledgling church in such a cosmopolitan setting would have found itself "tossed to and fro," always about to be carried away by a new idea, a strange doctrine, by a seductive culture.

In this sublime pastoral letter, the writer—was it St. Paul?—resorts to a metaphor that springs from the cardinal doctrine of the Christian faith, the Incarnation: the church moves through the world as the Body of Christ: "There is one body and one Spirit, just as you were called to the one hope that belongs to your call, one Lord, one faith, one baptism, one God and Father of us all, who is above all and through all and in all." The church will be able to hold together, maintaining "the unity of the Spirit in the bond of peace," and to find its way through the threatening world, as it remembers: "You are the body of Christ."

That leads us to rejoice in *our* diversity—in the variety of gifts we bring to the body—and to hold together, not in rigid conformity, but in organic connection to each other and to Christ, in whom it all coheres.

Here, in undeniable connection to each other in Christ, we are all together because we are baptized into Christ. We have the real possibility to speak the truth in love. You can see this here, this week; you can hear people speaking the truth in love. Wouldn't you agree?

Here we are, from a dozen seminaries diverse in history, liturgical practice, and even dogmatic expression. And we are, the seventy or so of us, as much a mosaic as our schools: in age, economic and social background, personal idiosyncrasies. But, we gather in these small rooms with their makeshift pulpits, open the Bible, and somehow find ways to speak to relative strangers about the things that matter most to us. Right there, in those sermon workshops, we hear it and see it, the reality in which we live: one Lord, one faith, one baptism. And there we have the real possibility to speak to each other in the kind of speech that leads us to grow up into the full stature of Christ.

We should be helped in this by the mere fact that Phillips Brooks walked among these trees, studied and preached right here. Think of it! You and I are here trying to learn to preach in the very place where our greatest American Anglican preacher labored over theology and church history and exegesis! We are certainly helped by the understanding of preaching to which his study and experience led him.

In the Lyman Beecher Lectures on preaching in 1877, Brooks gave an enduring definition of preaching: "Preaching is the bringing of truth through personality." Today he would probably choose the word "personhood," to suggest not only the essentially personal element of preaching, but also to emphasize the organic connection to the community of a Christian's daily life and speech. He wrote: "Preaching is the communication of truth by man to men." In the organic connection that is the Body of Christ—person to person—the Word of God is spoken and heard.[1]

Christian preaching, like Christianity itself, is a material matter—life in the flesh with people who are given their names and their corporate identity at a specific time and place, where babies cry and adults get wet, in Holy Baptism. This is where we speak to each other, the truth spoken in love—in the community of grace, forbearance, forgiveness, and hope.

Another great homiletician, H. H. Farmer, reminds us that preaching is *speech*, that the proclamation of the Word of God occurs in a moment of speaking and hearing among human beings at a particular time and place. The sound waves produced in the larynx of a person vibrate in the ear of the hearer, in a distinctively human moment, in what some would say is the most intimate human experience. The Gospel is spoken, person to person, larynx to eardrums. And there, in an experience so essential to being human that we take it for granted, lies the possibility of speaking the truth in love.

A guest of the Maori, the indigenous people of New Zealand, I was invited to take part in their annual New Year's festival. This four-day event combines ancient Maori ritual with Anglican liturgy: Most of the Maori are Anglicans. There is a long fast, a great feast, morning and evening prayer, and the ongoing deliberations of the community.

At this particular festival the community was faced with a difficult question: Would they put their sacred tradition—heretofore handed down as oral tradition—into writing? This discussion went on constantly on the green *marai* and out under the trees, and it took the form of both respectful argument and extensive storytelling.

We all slept together, lined up in sleeping bags, on the floor of the big, ornately carved meeting house. Hanging from a beam in the center of the house was a bare light bulb, with a cord attached. Anyone who wished to speak to the community—at any hour of the night—could simply turn on the light, get everyone's attention, and begin speaking.

So we lay in our beds, listening to a story or a thought that had come to someone at two in the morning. The question never came to a vote, and at the end of the meeting the Maori had decided simply to keep on meeting and eating and telling stories, to keep on talking. It was their own version of trying to speak the truth in love.

Two of my colleagues at Drew were delegates to the General Conference of the United Methodist Church. They came home quite discouraged, not so much by the actions that were taken—and not taken—at the conference as by the spirit of the meeting. Many had dug in their heels on this position or that long before the conference began, and there was excessive dependence upon caucusing and political maneuvering, not to mention unrestrained anger and a hateful spirit—about as far as one could get from Wesley's ways.

This, I suppose, should not surprise us. It seems that the larger the group the less successful we will be in speaking to each other both frankly and charitably, especially about things that matter most to us.

Isn't that so? I have worked among Methodists for more than thirty years; what I experience in a Methodist theological school and in Methodist congregations is in sharp contrast to the reports that have come from Cleveland.

For what it's worth, I was told by one of my Jewish colleagues that that there is a teaching in Judaism that matters of sexuality are best discussed in groups no larger than two!

So, how do we, as preachers and leaders in the church, find a way in our own vexed and volatile time to speak the truth in love?

So far, we Anglicans have done pretty well at this; we do have some advantages. We are not, by and large, preoccupied with doctrinal precision; most of us have been content to say the historic creeds in our common worship without pinning each other down on specifics. Also, we are not in the habit of hitting each other over the head with the Bible: We try to listen to the Bible with reverence and humility and to leave the authoritative teaching, finally, to the Holy Spirit's guidance.

These are great advantages, as a community tries to keep on talking about important things. But there is more: Our common life is centered around the table of our Lord. It is at the table that we hear the Scriptures read, listen to preaching, say our prayers, and seek forgiveness and reconciliation.

It is simply more likely that people of differing opinions will be able to stick together if they decide that what they have most in common is that they are all the guests of Christ, the head of the feast. Remembering a common baptism into the Body, and gathered around the table of the Lord, we have a better chance of keeping on talking as we try to speak the truth in love. And that could set all of our perplexing questions in the proper context, something like what you can see in the Maori people eating and telling their stories and sleeping together while confronting a tough question.

We might, then, whether we are up against questions of sexuality or social justice, meet those questions as people with a common identity and a common mission. That would be a great contribution to American Christianity in the twenty-first century, if we could keep ourselves reminded, as the writer to the Ephesians put is, that there *is*—whether, at our great denominational convocations, we act like it or not—one Lord, one faith, one baptism, and keep ourselves focused on him in whom the whole body is "joined and knit together," and aim at the apostle's lofty goal, that the church might "upbuild itself in love."

This is, of course, happening in parish churches, and monastic communities, and Christian homes, and even in practice preaching labs, where what causes us to speak to each other is also the goal of every word, to know among us the height and depth, the wisdom and power, of the love of God in Jesus Christ, our Lord.

Charles Rice is professor of homiletics at Drew University, Madison, New Jersey.

---

1. Phillips Brooks, *Lectures on Preaching* (Grand Rapids: Baker Book House, 1969. Reprinted from the 1907 Edition by E.P. Dutton Company, New York), p. 5.

THURSDAY IN THE SEVENTH WEEK OF EASTER

A Dangerous Business

Acts 22:30; 23:6–11
Hope H. Eakins

HAVE YOU ever considered what John Chrysostom and James Bond have in common? Well, they are both engaged in a dangerous business. Now, "preacher" doesn't rank right up there with other risky professions like "undercover cop" and "race car driver"; but I think it should, for if preaching has any power to convict, any power to change lives, then it is a dangerous business.

So when the Lord said, "Keep up your courage, Paul—you must bear witness also at Rome," Paul should have known what he was getting into. Any time the Lord says, "Take courage," it is time to look out. And, after all, trained in the Hebrew Scriptures at the feet of Gamaliel, Paul had certainly read how Jeremiah got himself tossed into a cistern for preaching words that God wanted him to say, but words that the people didn't want to hear. And while Paul was still calling himself Saul, he must have heard that Jesus was run out of town when he preached his first sermon in Nazareth. So it should have come as no surprise to Paul that his sermon in Jerusalem got him sent to prison and probably to his death in Rome.

That preaching is a dangerous business should come as no surprise to us either. After all, Jesus did not shrink from saying that he sends his disciples out as sheep in the midst of wolves, and Scripture does mention suffering for the sake of the gospel. But no matter how much preachers are warned that they are engaged in a dangerous business, they don't want it to be so. We figure that if we are delivering Good News the world should be thankful, and we should be rewarded.

Paul seemed to think so. Paul was like any other bright-eyed young curate, once he figured out whose side he was really on. He couldn't wait to tell the world the news that had changed his life. And as soon as he was commissioned to preach, he faced a magician named Elymas who challenged everything Paul was giving his life for. And Paul had the nerve to say to Elymas what preachers want to say to every vestry member who tells us that our sermons have offended the Altar Guild of Mrs. Major Donor, or the new folks or the old folks. Paul called Elymas a "son of the devil," and then saw to it that Elymas would see no more. It's a dangerous business, preaching. You can make enemies almost as soon as you begin.

Paul should have known the risk of preaching, and so should I. It was three or four years ago that I launched into a children's sermon about peace. "Jesus calls us ALL to be peacemakers," I concluded, and I asked the children what they could do to promote peace. They were wiggling on the chancel steps and swinging their feet and their eager little voices called out things like, "We could share our toys. We could not take things that don't belong to us." And with the audacity of God's little ones, "We could stop wars." Just as I was about to bless them and send them safely back to their pews, Haley Merrill raised her hand. Ah, I thought, we'll be truly blessed now to hear Haley for she is the intelligent and thoughtful child of fine parents who remove their television during Lent and worship in the front pew every Sunday. So, "Yes, Haley?" I inquired. "How can you be a peacemaker?" And Haley answered: "When I want peace, I just call downstairs and say, 'Would you two please stop fighting! I'm trying to get some sleep!'"

Preaching is a dangerous business because the Gospel is a dangerous text. Paul was arrested because he refused to water down the Good News. He did not preach the Gospel as an amendment to Greek philosophy, a supplement to Judaism, or the beginning of another Jewish sect. He preached Christ crucified as an assault upon the earth, a mind-shaking, gut-wrenching overthrowing of the common perspective. Paul wasn't so much interested in what the Pharisees and Sadducees thought about the resurrection of the body as he was in declaring that Jesus' resurrection rolled away a stone from more than a tomb. That our lives would never be the same again, because Jesus brought new life, Risen Life.

Paul did not shrink from declaring the full Gospel of God, and his passion drove him to engage the Pharisees and Sadducees in dialogue; he became a Jew in order to tell God's story to Jews. Just as he became weak to win the weak; and to those outside the law, he became as one outside the law. Paul preached to people in a context and a tongue they could each understand, but he didn't get co-opted by their cultures; his voice didn't get lost in their voice. He knew the truth, and spoke it in their language; he walked the narrow line where his voice could be heard because it came from his heart.

Too often preachers fail to communicate because they sound like foreigners speaking a language called Ecclesiastican. "Tourist preaching," Fred Buechner calls it, the belief that if preachers speak the truth "loudly and distinctly and slowly enough their congregations will understand them."[1] I am reading *The Poisonwood Bible* now, the story of a Baptist missionary named Nathan Price who is a tourist preacher in Africa. He insists that to be saved, the Africans must be baptized in the Kwilu River, but the Africans know better. They won't go where the crocodiles go, so they stay away not only from the river but from the Gospel. Nathan keeps on preaching, louder and louder, but he doesn't win any converts.

It ought to be clear to us that church words are not working well in today's world. "Conversion" is how we move DOS files to a Mac format; "election" is what happens in November, "Grace" is a rock star, and "justification" is making text even on a computer screen. But if faith comes by hearing and hearing comes by preaching, then those who would declare the Good News have to find new ways to say that *conversion* is finding the grace to stop following our own nose to destruction. And *grace* is being loved, just because you're you. And *justification* means that God wants to have a relationship with us, and *election* means that God chooses us and gives us a job to do.

The opposite of preaching in a language foreign to the listener is preaching in language so familiar that it has no power. In the attempt to be relevant, you become relevant to nothing that matters, offering no more than moral incentive or the gospel of prosperity. There is a church near home in Connecticut that once offered a preaching series on Lent entitled L-E-N-T = Let's Eliminate Negative Thinking. I suppose it can be done. I suppose you can avoid the danger of mentioning the bloody cross. You can skip right over the death part and get to the good bit about how "the green blade riseth." You can avoid the danger and get to the positive thinking. But Jesus came to tell us that no amount of positive thinking can save us—and that's okay because we have a Savior.

It is not always very dangerous to preach to the same congregation week after week. You get to know them, to know the concerns of the community, to decide whether it is time to afflict the comfortable or to comfort the afflicted. You can even preach a little heresy now and then, because if you overdo God's mercy one Sunday, you can emphasize God's justice the next. You don't have to be good Anglicans speaking carefully crafted sentences that balance each declaration with another one that begins, "Yet on the other hand." You can be a one-handed preacher. You can take risks; you can live dangerously. You can leave God's people with holy questions and not with pat answers.

The problem in preaching to the same congregation is that you can forget that preaching is a dangerous business, forget to live on the edge and proclaim the Word with boldness. When they whine about "Manna, Manna, Manna," you can get seduced into placating their hunger with a designer menu instead of the bread of life.

Last week, two sisters at the Lynn Lucas Middle School in Houston, Texas, went to school with more than their textbooks in their book bags. Bibles they had, and when their teacher discovered them, she enforced the law against religious texts in school. She wrenched the books from the girls' grasp, hurled them into the garbage and sent the young women to the principal for discipline. Oh, that we were so blessed! Oh, that our congregations believed that the power of Scripture is so great as to threaten them! Oh, that we felt the shudder of preaching a powerful word with boldness! For if our knees do not knock as we step into the pulpit, if our preaching is only a matter of exposition and encouragement, then we will not be faithful preachers of Christ and him crucified and risen for us.

As Paul was driven across the sea of Adria, lashed by a storm, without a mast or a star to steer by, he did two things. He knelt on the wet deck and prayed. And then, getting up, he took the last bread on board; and he blessed it, and broke it, and gave thanks for it. And after the crew had shared this holy meal, they escaped to dry land. It was worth the storm and worth the tempest, for Paul went on to preach with boldness and freedom, knowing that, though he was in a dangerous business, he was not alone; and that, in his danger, there was great joy.

Hope H. Eakins is rector of St. John's Church,
Essex, Connecticut.

---

1. Frederick Buechner, *Whistling in the Dark: An ABC Theologized* (New York: Harper & Row), 1988, p. 107.

EVENING PRAYER

A Life Worthy of the Calling

Ephesians 4:17–32
Joy E. Rogers

E-MAIL FROM Roger carried the glad tidings that I would preach the fourteenth sermon you will hear today. Lucky me. The accompanying lectionary appointed a passage from Ephesians for tonight's liturgy with a subtitle: Moral Injunctions. Lucky you.

Under the circumstances, I considered a little-used homiletical strategy called brevity. Another approach I contemplated involved graphic and imaginative descriptions of the licentiousness to which the Gentiles have abandoned themselves.

But it occurs to me that the challenge this evening for both this preacher and her hearers is not such an unusual one. "The Word became flesh," and ever since, preachers have spent time and energy turning the truth of an incarnate God back into words. Week in and week out, we add our words to a wordy world. We dare to talk to people who have been nearly talked to death, by advertisers, and news media, by bosses and spouses and kids, by teachers, and relatives and clients and customers. Even by each other.

We offer words to a people who are more and more attuned to visual stimulation and sound bites than to sustained verbal arguments. For us, as for the ancient letter writer, the words we speak already carry a label for many folk because, for many people in our pews, "moral injunctions" is a synonym for a sermon. It makes one wonder if anyone is hearing a word we say.

A preacher matters—I believe that. But a preacher is not enough, because words are not enough. The writer of Ephesians began this chapter exhorting his readers: ". . . I beg you to lead a life worthy of the calling to which you have been called."

It is easy to forget that baptismal lives, or these precious vocations, are not our own bright ideas. We are here—at this worship service, at this conference, part of this problematic institution called church—because we are called, by a Lord who was willing to die for the privilege of issuing such a call to the likes of us.

"You did not choose me; I chose you."

A life worthy of the calling. The letter writer takes the rest of the chapter to tell us what he thinks that looks like. I am as resistant as anyone to the "shoulds" and "oughts" of moral injunctions. To dreary notions of duty and discipline, imposed by holier-than-thou-types, and backed up by threats of eternal damnation. However, I find that I am drawn to the notion of *a life worthy of the calling.*

All the good words by all the good preachers who have enriched my imagination, stretched my soul, and confronted my heart with God's own truth would never have gotten anywhere with me if there had not been someone to show me what "a life worthy of the calling" looked like. A chapter of almost shrill moral injunctions starts to echo with deeper sounds and more compelling resonances. Memory clothes stern words with a vivid image of what they might look like all dressed up with some place to go.

My grandmother was a Victorian matron. A handsome woman of elegant bearing, strong convictions, and boundless energy. From the time I was old enough to clamber unaided onto buses and trolley cars, my grandmother regularly appeared on our doorstep to collect me to accompany her on an amazing assortment of visitations and errands. We did churches, lots of them, always Episcopal: Choral Matins, Solemn Evensongs, Healing Liturgies, even Adoration of the Blessed Sacrament.

"For surely you have heard about [Christ] and were taught in him. . . . You were taught to put away your former way of life . . . and to be renewed in the spirit of your minds. . . ."

My grandmother knew someone everywhere, and she always presented herself and me to the presiding clergy at the end of the service. I retain three important learnings from those expeditions. 1) God, like my grandmother, apparently liked hats a lot and she kept me well supplied. 2) Whatever identified Episcopalians as a distinct denomination, it had nothing to do with similar styles of worship. 3) Anglicans seemed to take some delight in the idiosyncratic personalities of their clergy. They were all a bit odd. (That is no longer the case.)

". . . Clothe yourselves with the new self, created according to the likeness of God in true righteousness and holiness."

We made rounds of friends and acquaintances, morning coffee with Mrs. Jones, who kept a home for her grown but daft son. Afternoon tea with the elderly McGilvray sisters, Irene, Rose and Bessie. Fortunately, protocol decreed that I address them all as "Miss" McGilvray since I never could tell one from the other.

"So then, putting away falsehood, let all of us speak the truth to our neighbors, for we are members of one another."

We took meals to the sick, carried cakes to the grieving, and visited the dying in nursing homes. We did weddings and wakes.

"Let no evil talk come out of your mouths, but only what is useful for building up, as there is need, so that your words may give grace to those who hear."

We made annual pilgrimages to Philadelphia's sacred historic sites, including that early feminist shrine, the house of Betsy Ross. We didn't go as tourists. I always felt my grandmother was checking up on the caretakers, making sure the hallowed places were being adequately kept up. The crack in the bell bothered her a lot.

"Be angry but do not sin; do not let the sun go down on your anger, and do not make room for the devil."

Some afternoons we stopped at the hospital so I could help her stock the little cart that she would push through the corridors the next day as the hospital auxiliary volunteer. We placed flowers on the graves of long-departed relatives. We took baby garments to a young woman that some sailor had gotten in trouble and then abandoned. It was years before I figured out the connection between baby booties and absent sailors. (There is the graphic example of licentiousness.)

"Put away from you all bitterness and wrath and anger and wrangling and slander, together with all malice, and be kind to one another, tenderhearted, forgiving one another, as God in Christ has forgiven you."

A life worthy of the calling. Not a list of rules, not a dreary recital of moral injunctions; but a complicated web of relationships. Relationships that encompassed activities and attitudes, even clothes, food, and words. Please and thank you. Hats and gloves. Stand up straight. Wash your hands. Presence, manners, posture, hygiene, work, and prayer.

The rules were clearly there. But equally clear, they were derivative. Something more drove this regimen. My grandmother did not much care for the old Prayer of Humble Access that still graces the Rite I service: *We are not worthy so much as to pick up the crumbs under thy table.* To my grandmother, the very notion of crumbs under the table was already an affront to the way God intended the world to work.

I was sometimes daunted by this imposing authority figure; she was not a user-friendly grandma, this spiritual arbiter for her family, church, and community, but I have no memories of resenting her strenuous ministrations on my behalf. Something more than duty was at work in these lessons in discipleship.

My first school was in a city neighborhood, only blocks from my grandparents' home. We first-graders tumbled out its doors for recess on every clear day, for fifteen minutes of relative freedom on a giant slab of concrete surrounded by a large iron fence. It never struck me as peculiar that my grandmother's regular daily walk brought her to that fence at precisely the time of our release. But she was there. Waiting, watching, a silent wave if our eyes met, then on with her walk.

I was loved. I knew it. It showed. In a plaid dress, with skinny legs and scraped knees, I was held, then and always, by a gaze that required nothing more of me than my sheer existence and by a presence that found my presence sheer delight. And if a Victorian grandmother was not capable of perfect love, of truly unconditional love, it was close enough. The rest was derivative. Not coercive power to remake a child in her own image. But an offering, a self-giving of what she understood as the best she had in her to call forth the best in me.

I responded not out of fear, not yet knowing myself capable of either duty or love, but because I simply received love freely given, and because I wanted to be like her. I still do. I buy my own hats now.

A life worthy of the calling founded upon a relationship, one of authority and care, of discipline and delight. A covenant that held us both, a covenant in which to grow old or grow up, but always, always to grow—in knowledge, and service, and love.

There is a vision of a church—a grandmotherly realm of presence, manners, posture, hygiene, work, and prayer; a realm of derivative rules and a regimen driven by something more; a church on a mission to mold human beings into Christ's likeness; a church that will love all people into Christ's presence. A church full of graced lives that enflesh moral injunctions with gospel presence—people who transform shoulds and oughts into a joy-filled dance of life and love and God; the people who preach the sermons that we see and touch and taste and wonder at, long before we are ready to hear (let alone speak) the word that will come from a pulpit; even those who, even now, are Good News for us when we are overwhelmed by a wordy world. Even us, even now, before we ever say a word.

Lives worthy of the calling—maybe they look like Moses or David or Paul or Eldad and Medad; or Janice Robinson's parents, or Wallace Stegner's mother, or Bill Eakins's Miss Pfost. Or Nicholas, Linda Clader's favorite saint.

Words are never enough, preachers! You are more than your words. Words weren't enough for God. The Word became flesh and lived among us. To make a covenant with us to call forth our best, by the self-giving of God, even to death on a cross.

I beg you to live a life worthy of the calling to which you have been called.

Not because we're so good, but because we're God's. Not because we're always faithful, just forgiven. Not because it's safe, just saving. Not because it was our own bright idea, but because God has work for us to do, even words for us to say. Not holier *than* thou, but holy *like* thou, and holy *with* thou, like Moses and David and my grandmother and my God. Because we are loved and we know it and it shows. And because we want to be like him.

Joy E. Rogers is rector of St. Thomas's Church, Battle Creek, Michigan.

FEAST OF COLUMBA

Traveling Day

1 Corinthians 3:11–23; Luke 10:17–20
David J. Schlafer

THIS IS a traveling day—no question about it. Bags are packed; engines are running. We are all but out of here! There is a pause, brief but sincere, in which we turn, and say, with feeling: "Thank you so much; you've been just great!" to everyone in *this* seminary community who has done so much to shape for us a welcome space this week. It's hard to go, of course. But it's *time*. Deep inside, a little song is doing a frolic: *I'm leaving on a jet plane / Don't know when I'll be back again!* This is a traveling day.

We are going home, most of us. But where IS home, really? The majority of folks hopping a jet to what they *now* call "home" were *leaving* home to head for seminary not so very long ago. And what you are going back to, today, won't be home for long. Those who enter ordained ministry quickly discover that they don't get to "settle down" after they leave seminary. Unsettling though it may be to entertain the notion, the fact of the matter is that we aren't likely to get the chance to put deep roots down anywhere—ever. With occasional exceptions, ordained ministers are itinerant preachers. They never get to settle down. I was a preacher's kid. I remember my mother, hearing from my dad that we were heading off for yet another "field of service," and muttering to herself: "The story of my life—*pick up and move!*"

She felt, I think (and so did I), that this was a particular burden for a minister's family—"a cross we had to bear," so to speak. But that is not so. "Pick up and move," is the story of every human life—certainly of every Christian life. But it's not an easy truth to travel with. I can hear the groaning and complaining of St. Columba's monks, as they moved from one missionary outpost to another: "Are we THERE YET, Columba? When are we *ever* going to settle down? We don't really *have a home!*"

"Pick up and move," however, means more than constantly having to change the place you hang your toothbrush. Returning to their base camp, the disciples of Jesus are ecstatic. They have discovered a place of permanence much more stable than any geographical location! They have returned from a mission that has confirmed their ministerial competence, their excellence in exorcism. "Lord!" they chortle, "even the demons are subject to us!" Having plunged into daunting territory, they have persevered, and discovered, in the risky process, a permanent, portable identity—"Powerful Preacher!" Jesus will be *so* proud!

Jesus acknowledges their authority (not surprising, since he conferred it on them in the first place!), and agrees with them that they *will* work wonders. But then—in a heartbeat—he shifts gears. He seems to all but dismiss what they've done—blow it off. "Don't rejoice in this, that the spirits submit to you," he says. "Rather, that your names are written in heaven." I envision these itinerant preachers plunging headlong into vertigo. "What in the *world* does THAT mean? Aren't we THERE YET, Jesus? How much LONGER is it gonna be?"

It's all very well for us preachers to talk, in abstract terms, about "the firm foundation" we proclaim that is "Jesus Christ." Yet it's easy to forget that St. Paul makes that observation initially in a fractured, conflicted parish setting where several different preachers were setting forth their own respective versions of just such a "firm foundation." As preachers, we are never given the luxury of settling down into a stable form of doctrine, method, vision, practice. We never grasp the "firm foundation"—the Firm Foundation grasps us—and continually picks us up and moves us along.

"I don't know anyone who is an expert in preaching," Barbara Brown Taylor told us in her presentations this week. What? Doesn't she know *herself*? Well, yes, I think she *does*. "Every idea we form of God, God must, in mercy, shatter." That was the experience of C. S. Lewis. I suspect, if we are given the grace to be at all honest—and a bit brave—that this is what we will find to be the story of our preaching lives as well.

Pick up and move, itinerant preachers! This is a traveling day.

Go with God.

David J. Schlafer is coeditor of this volume.

On This Rock

Matthew 16:13–23
Barbara Brown Taylor

SO YOU are the ones. I wondered who you would turn out to be. A couple of years ago, when Jim Waits first started reviving the Fund for Theological Education, he told me who he was looking for: the brightest and best possible candidates for ministry—people with brains, heart, faith, and character—who might be persuaded to work long hours for low pay, if they had any idea how vital their vocations might turn out to be. He was looking for people who might save the church, although he would never have put it that way. Only God can save the church, and yet God has from the beginning chosen to do that by choosing certain people and asking them to take the lead. Sometimes the asking is spectacular— burning bushes, descending doves, that kind of thing—but far more often it is as ordinary as someone saying, "Have you ever thought about becoming a minister? I think you'd be good at it." Sometimes it even comes through the mail, in the form of a letter from some outfit down in Atlanta that wants to give you money to go to seminary.

You are the ones. Whatever you decide to do about it, you have been invited to consider vocations in the church, and already you are getting a taste of the high expectations. How are your grades? Your prayer life? Are you managing to keep up with your servanthood as well as your studies? Have people begun to apologize to you if they say a curse word in your presence? In this vocation, the currency is not technical skill or billable hours. The currency is the quality of your life. It is how much of the Christ people see when they look at you. That is because the church survives by sacraments—by outward and visible signs of inward and spiritual graces—which include not only water, bread, and wine, but also men and women who are willing to live in a certain way. Creatures of flesh, we learn best by flesh. Our bodies are primary sources of revelation for us, and God knows that, if nothing else works to get our attention, then what happens in our bodies will often do the trick. Cool water on a hot day, the weight of a sleeping child against the chest, food shared with strangers, a pounding heart in the middle of the night—these are the things that make theologians out of us. Our struggle to make meaning out of them is what fuels our search for God, and that is why the church needs sacraments. Sacraments allow us to contemplate all that we cannot see by contemplating what we can.

Some churches count two sacraments and some count seven, but the number is not as important as the pattern. Once we have learned to recognize God's presence in Holy Communion, then we are better equipped to recognize God's presence wherever bread is taken, blessed, broken, and given. Once we have learned to recognize God's gift of new life in holy baptism, then we are better equipped to recognize that gift wherever water flows to cleanse and refresh.

Last week I took part in a celebration of Holy Communion with people from many different faith traditions. When it came time to pass the bread around the circle, I watched Baptists feed Presbyterians who fed Episcopalians who fed Methodists. When the bread came to the one Quaker in the group, he smiled at the woman holding the loaf, put his hand on her shoulder, and stepped back so that she could feed the next person in the circle. He put his hand on that person's shoulder too, so that the circle was unbroken even though he did not eat the bread. Watching him, I remembered what another Quaker taught me years ago. "How do you survive without sacraments?" I asked him. "Oh, we have a sacrament," he said, "a very powerful one. It is the sacrament of another human being. When we look into one another's faces, that is our bread and wine, our constant reminder that God is with us."

It is a sacrament all Christians share, whether we count it or not. Over and over again, when human beings have asked the invisible God to come out of hiding, God has said, "You're not up to it, I promise, but I will give you a reasonable facsimile. Here is a neighbor, someone just like you. Treat her as you would treat me. Give him whatever you want to give me, and trust that I have received the gift."

For better or worse, clergy provide congregations with lots of opportunities to practice this sacrament of another human being in a particularly focused way. If someone is furious with God, then clergy make great punching bags. If someone is grateful to God, then clergy may come to work and find homemade pound cakes or jelly jars full of wildflowers sitting in front of their doors. It goes with the territory, since churches survive by sacraments and clergy tend to be identified as the most sacramental persons around.

If you decide to go ahead and do this, then your parishioners are going to watch *everything* you do—the way we you run a meeting, the way you hold a baby, how fast you drive your car and whether you bite your fingernails. It is because you will have become their parson—their representative person—who stands on the tipsy edge between God and God's people, having promised to be true to them both. People will watch you to see what a life of faith really looks like. They will watch you because they want to see Jesus, or at least one of Jesus' best friends.

Living this sacramental life turns out to be quite a job description, and depending on your personality it can make you or break you. I belong to a large circle of friends who occasionally suffer from what psychologists call "impostor's syndrome." Maybe you will recognize the symptoms too. It comes on you when you are in some gathering of people who start telling you how wonderful you are—how full of promise you are, what an inspiration you are, how they hope all of their children will grow up to be just like you. No matter how hard you have worked to earn accolades like that, you start feeling a little damp under your arms. Little bees start buzzing around inside your head and whatever modest, accommodating thing you happen to be saying back to the person in front of you, there is a cartoon balloon over your head with what you are really thinking inside of it: "I have somehow gotten in here by mistake, and I need to get out of here as soon as I can before someone discovers who I really am and asks me to leave."

If this sounds at all familiar, then you too have impostor's syndrome. High achievers are especially susceptible. Ministerial candidates are doomed. That is why I asked Simon Peter to be with us here today—Simon son of Jonah, nicknamed Rocky, who in ten short verses of Matthew's Gospel goes from cornerstone of the church to satanic stumbling block, and all for the love of Jesus. The story of his rise and fall is a lot longer in Matthew than it is in Mark or Luke, and it is not a story about recognizing who Jesus really is. That happened earlier, in the fourteenth chapter, when Jesus stilled the storm and saved Peter from drowning, and everyone in the boat worshipped him, saying, "Truly you are the Son of God."

As far as Matthew is concerned, Jesus' identity has already been established. He is the son of God, and his disciples know it. What has not yet been established is the identity of the church. Once Jesus has used up his body and ascended into heaven, what sacramental presence will remain on earth? What kind of body will the church be, and what kind of virtues will its leaders embody?

There were at least twelve people present when Jesus began to investigate the answers to these questions. "Who do people say that the Son of Man is?" he asked them. Were the disciples listening to the people? Did they know how to read people's hungers by the foods they named? John the Baptist, his disciples answered him, Elijah or Jeremiah. Those are names chosen by people who are ravenous for change. "Good," Jesus said, "so you heard them. The church needs to know how to listen to the people."

"But who do you say that I am?" he asked them next. Did the disciples also know how to listen to God? Not to their own experience, although that was important; and not to their own reason, although that was important too—but to the still, small voice of God inside of them. Did they know how to recognize that voice?

"You are the Messiah, the Son of the living God," Peter blurted out, and Jesus blessed him on the spot. Jesus made Peter the subject of his own little beatitude, but like all of the other beatitudes this one had a surprise ending. "Blessed are you, Simon son of Jonah!" *Lucky, lucky you!* "For flesh and blood has not revealed this to you, but my Father in heaven." *For you did not come up with this answer on your own.* So good again, Peter. You heard God. The church needs to know how to listen to God.

According to Matthew, that was enough to convince Jesus that Peter could be trusted with the keys to the kingdom. If Peter knew how to listen to all the voices in and around him—and if he could still tell which one was the voice of God—then he would not get too far lost for long. People could say whatever they said around him: good, bad, or ugly. He would listen, but he would not get bowled over. As rock of the church, Peter's chief virtue was that he knew the sound of God.

And in the next moment he forgot it. The moment Jesus started talking about the inevitability of his own suffering and death, Peter clamped his hands over his ears. "God forbid it, Lord!" he rebuked Jesus (he rebuked *Jesus*!), "This must never happen to you!" And just like that, Peter the Rock became Satan the Stumbling Block, because he got his own voice confused with the voice of God.

It was just a little slip. Jesus did not take the keys away from Peter, or change his name to "Pebble." Peter remained in the inner circle along with James and John, one of the three people Jesus wanted with him when things got especially intense. Peter was only Satan for a second, when he forgot the sound of God. Then he remembered it again. Then he forgot it again. Then he remembered it again, and who knows how many times the cycle repeated itself after Matthew blew out the candle and closed his book.

On one hand, Jesus' choice of Peter seems almost ironic, a kind of sad parable about the true identity of the church: remembering, forgetting, remembering, forgetting. "Though all become deserters because of you, I will never desert you." Jesus of Nazareth? "I do not know the man" (Matt. 26:72b).

On the other hand, Jesus' choice of Peter seems a gesture of pure compassion. We are all far more like Peter than we are like Jesus, after all. If Peter is our model, then no one ever has to suffer from impostor's syndrome. God knows who we are. God has known us all along, and is still willing to trust us with the church—not because we are capable of drumming up much excellence on our own but because we are willing to keep remembering what we keep forgetting, and to keep listening for that voice that rings above the rest. Like Peter, our chief virtue is that we know the sound of God.

When I was contemplating ordination twenty-five years ago, I found a wise and moody priest whose name could have been Peter. The poor man was crawling with seminarians. We were all over him like flies on honey, because he seemed to have the right word for each one of us. Sometimes we pestered him so badly that he had to slam doors in our faces and tell us to *go away*. The first time he yelled at me I thought I would slide to the floor and die right there. Then he took me into his kitchen and fed me leftover Chinese. I adored him, which was hard on him, I know. One day I told him that my biggest fear about ordination was the perfection thing—impersonating Jesus in front of a whole lot of people who would see right through me—and he said, "Oh, lovey, that's not your job. If you decide to do this, then you're not promising to be perfect. You're just consenting to be visible—to let other people watch you while you try to figure our what real life is all about." Remembering, forgetting, remembering, forgetting.

What rock could be a better sacrament than a flawed and sometimes faithless rock? Who could leave more room for God to be God? And what better outward and visible sign of God's inward and spiritual grace could there be than a man or a woman who gets it right, and then gets it wrong and keeps on trying to *get it*—visibly, in front of a whole lot of people who are trying to do the same thing?

So you are the ones—the brightest and best possible candidates for ministry, the ones with brains, heart, faith, and character enough to shore up a sagging church? Well, do I have good news for you! You are not Jesus. No, you are Peter's children—sons and daughters of the rock on whom Christ has built the church, so that even the gates of Hades will not prevail against it.

Glory to God, whose power, working in us, can do infinitely more than we can ask or imagine. Glory to God from generation to genera-tion in the church, and in Christ Jesus forever and ever.

Barbara Brown Taylor is Harry R. Butman Professor of Religion and Philosophy at Piedmont College, Clarkesville, Georgia. She delivered this sermon at the Fund for Theological Education's Summer Conference in June, 2000, shortly after her presentations at the Preaching Excellence Conference.